CLICK FOR JOY!
QUESTIONS AND ANSWERS FROM CLICKER TRAINERS AND THEIR DOGS

by Melissa C. Alexander

with a foreword by Robert Bailey

Published by Sunshine Books, Inc.,
47 River Street, Suite 3
Waltham, MA 02453
781-398-0754
www.clickertraining.com

ISBN 1-890948-12-8
Printed in the United States of America

Library of Congress Number: 2002116878

9 8 7 6 5 4 3 2 1

This book is available at quantity discounts for multiple-copy purchases
For information call 1-800-47CLICK

Contents

Foreword

It was Karen Pryor who popularized the term and the practice of clicker training. Her 1985 book, *Don't Shoot the Dog,* captured the public's interest, and its appearance inadvertently led to a widespread assumption that clicker training was new. In fact, as Pryor herself explained in the introduction to her book, clicker training is based on the science and technology of operant conditioning and has been used since the 1940s.

Harvard psychologist, B. F. (Fred) Skinner and his colleague, Fred Keller, began discussing how to change everyday behavior in the late 1920s. Skinner published his landmark book *Behavior of Organisms* in 1938, wherein he described, in excruciating detail, how rats respond to environmental change under very controlled conditions. Skinner's work was not simple, and in fact, the book was boring. For a decade or so, few outside the field knew anything about the science of behaviorism. But meanwhile, two of Skinner's students, Keller and Marian Breland, began applying operant conditioning as a practical training method in 1943. They made their own clickers and trained many animals, from cockroaches to parakeets to dogs. By 1948, they had a growing business. Within ten years, they had spread the use of applied operant conditioning to cats, dolphins, parrots, sheep, cattle, raccoons, and dozens of other species.

Perhaps more importantly, the Brelands were teaching people the new technology. If you've seen animal shows at Marineland, Sea World, Busch Gardens, Six Flags, or dozens of other places, you've seen the Brelands' handiwork. The Brelands taught the trainers who trained the animals for the first shows at most of these places. These trainers, in turn, have passed the technology on to others. I was in that first wave of Breland students. I believe I learned my lessons well. I applied what I learned.

Some might point out, correctly, that Skinner had other students who also entered the animal training field. These students, however, had only a limited impact on animal trainers. Why? Because they missed a key message: simplicity. The Brelands knew how to make the technology work, and they knew how to teach others to make the technology work. They taught that behavior was naturally complicated, and that the trainer's job was to break apart behavior and make it simple. The Brelands were the first applied animal psychologists. They were also what are now called behavior analysts.

The Brelands were consultants to the US Navy Marine Mammal Program at Pt. Mugu, California. I was the program's first director of training. By 1965, I had left the Navy program and joined the Brelands. Several years after Keller died, Marian and I married. Marian died in September of 2001, but the simple, clear, and useful technology of operant conditioning, or clicker training, lives on through the successful efforts of others, including Melissa Alexander.

There are many books available purporting to describe clicker training, or some variant. Few of these books combine simplicity, readability, accuracy, and usefulness. Melissa has done well on all counts. Melissa describes basic principles, but eschews the many "rules" set forth by some other authors. (Marian and I always had trouble with these so-called "rules" because we violated most of them on a daily basis.)

I will admit to pleasure in reading Melissa's clear restatement of what Marian and I taught in our workshops and what we wrote on various Internet forums. I particularly appreciated Melissa's reference to our mantra, "Training is a mechanical skill." Furthermore, if you read carefully, you will learn about the aspects of reinforcement we called "timing, criteria, rate." Finally, and most wonderfully, she describes and discusses fluency, including the requirement of rate or performance speed.

The majority of trainers Marian and I have observed do not teach the concept of fluency or understand its role in training. We always used fluency to build response strength, or rate of response; only sometimes did we add the power of variable reinforcement schedules to build even greater response strength. We found that training to the point of fluency provides responses sufficiently strong for any but the most extreme of behaviors and circumstances.

A few words about writing style: Melissa is refreshingly detailed in her definitions and descriptions of procedures. In my personal opinion, technical and "how–to" descriptions should leave little to the reader's imagination, but some modern writers and editors have pushed succinctness to the point where prose becomes cryptic, leaving much too much to interpretation. Students and practitioners seeking information on definitions or procedures need more information, not less.

This book is written from the perspective of a dog trainer. However, using only a little imagination, a trainer can easily apply the technology described here to work with virtually any animal. *Click for Joy: Questions and Answers from Clicker Trainers and their Dogs* will be a good resource for anyone applying operant technology to change the behavior of animals. I recommend it not only to dog trainers, but also to trainers in zoos and aquaria and to animal trainers doing stage or theater work.

— Robert Bailey

Introduction

In 1998, I stumbled onto clicker training during a Web search. I had long been interested in dog training, and this science-based method appealed to the intellect in me. The more I read, the more interested I became. To test it out, I dragged my eight-year-old Great Pyrenees out of retirement. Satch had been traditionally trained as a puppy but hadn't seemed to enjoy it, so we had settled for polite house manners.

I began by using the clicker to teach him to touch the end of a target stick with his nose, a behavior unlike anything he had ever done before. Touch, click, treat. Touch, click, treat. After a few repetitions a light went on in his eyes. He got it—and he loved it. Everything he learned through clicker training he did enthusiastically and quickly. But if I asked for a behavior he had learned as a puppy, the light would go out of his eyes and he would revert to the slow, deliberate movement characteristic of a "giant breed." I finally understood what the term "shut down" really means.

I was sold. At that time, books and videos on clicker training were scarce. I bought what I could, but most of my education came from online mailing lists. I got to brainstorm with experienced trainers and newbies alike—and I learned from both. As time passed, I learned that not all of the experienced trainers I had been emulating practiced what they preached. Many seemed to believe in the technology only to a certain point, at which they abandoned their positive message in favor of corrections. Fortunately, at that time I joined the Association of Pet Dog Trainers and was privileged to meet some of the most respected trainers in the world—people like Karen Pryor, Ian Dunbar, Deb Jones, and most importantly, Bob and Marian Bailey.

I am, without apology, a Bailey devotee. Over the course of forty-five years, the Baileys and their staff at Animal Behavior Enterprises, which Marian and her first husband, Keller Breland, founded, trained fifteen thousand animals of a hundred and forty different species, including dogs. Scientists-turned-business people, the Baileys needed the most efficient and effective method of training they could find. In some of their projects, such as training trip-wire detection dogs in Vietnam, human lives quite literally depended on the reliability of their training. The method they chose was the very same one I discuss in this book. Although they call themselves operant conditioning trainers rather than clicker trainers, they used primarily positive reinforcement, extinction, and (to a far lesser degree) negative punishment to achieve their goals. They resorted to positive punishment only a dozen times in four and a half decades. In my mind, the Baileys and their staff had proven over and over what operant conditioning and clicker training could accomplish. If they could do it, I—or anyone else—could do it too.

In June of 1999, I made another life-changing decision. I had become increasingly disenchanted with the prevalent discussion and recommendation of physical corrections and other punishment-based solutions found on the Internet mailing lists I was on. When Debbie Otero, a then-beginning clicker trainer and pet owner from Florida, asked me to start a new list, I was initially reluctant to put in that much time and effort. However, when she promised to help—and when I realized that without a new list people new to clicker training would believe that corrections were an accepted or necessary part of training—I agreed, and ClickerSolutions was born.

I was told more than once that no one would want to restrict himself or herself to positive solutions—that this list was doomed to fail. But ClickerSolutions grew, and as of June 2002 it has over 2600 members. I receive notes from members on a regular basis, thanking me for providing such a safe, positive forum. What those people don't realize is that I've gotten at least as much from ClickerSolutions as they have. I have learned from and been inspired by the members, beginners and experienced alike, and I've made many friends.

It doesn't take too long readings postings on a mailing list to realize the same questions are asked again and again. It also doesn't take long to realize that the answers to those questions frequently conflict, even those posted by experienced trainers. Ironically, even seemingly contradictory answers are frequently each "right"—they just aren't complete. Techniques that give desirable short-term results can sometimes have undesirable long-term consequences. The more I learned, the more I wanted to make sure people got more complete answers to common questions, so they could make educated choices. So I decided to compile those questions and write answers based on the cumulative experience of many trainers. My friend Doug Johnson, who knows more about applying operant conditioning principles to dog training than anyone I've ever met, offered to be my technical reader. Karen Pryor and the lovely people at Sunshine Books offered to publish the book.

Click for Joy: Questions and Answers from Clicker Trainers and their Dogs is the result. This is not a step-by-step manual, nor is it an exhaustive source of information on any particular aspect of training. It is intended as a reference guide to put the answers to your questions at your fingertips. I've included cross-references and an index to help you find your way around, a glossary of behavioral terms, and a list of other resources that I recommend. I hope you enjoy reading it as much as I have enjoyed writing it.

— Melissa C. Alexander

CHAPTER 1 About Clicker Training

What is Clicker Training?

Clicker training is both a technology for training animals— in this book we will focus on dogs—and a training philosophy.

As a technology, clicker training relies on *positive reinforcement* rather than coercion or punishment. As in other positive methods, the trainer reinforces a desired behavior with something the dog likes or wants. Positive reinforcement makes it more likely that the dog will repeat the behavior in the future.

Two things, however, make clicker training unique.

Will it work for my dog? **page 4**

What is operant conditioning?
page 178

Are clicker training and operant conditioning the same thing? **page 181**

see also

- First, its practitioners emphasize the science underlying the method. Clicker training is based on the principles of *operant* and *classical conditioning*. This makes clicker training more than a method, more than a set of step-by-step recipes to get behavior. Clicker trainers who learn the underlying principles have at their disposal a powerful set of tools that enable them to analyze behaviors, modify existing methods for individual animals, and create new methods where none previously existed.

- Second, as the trainer you use a marker signal, the clicker, to tell the animal when he does what you want. The clicker is like a camera "taking a picture" of the behavior you are training for.

The technology is, at its core, very simple:

1. Get the behavior.

2. Mark the behavior.

3. Reinforce the behavior.

For example, say you want to teach your dog to sit. When he sits, you click. Then you give him a bite of his favorite treat. The click means "That behavior right there! That's what I want!" and "You've earned a reward." If you click and reinforce every time your dog sits, he will soon figure out that sitting earns a treat and offer the sit more often. You can then add a cue, "sit," to tell him when you want him to do the behavior.

More importantly, clicker training is more than using a clicker to train your dog. It's a different way of thinking, a way of relating to animals that creates a partnership that is mutually reinforcing and pleasurable. As a philosophy, clicker training has evolved from the works and ideas of Karen Pryor, Jean Donaldson, Bob and Marian Bailey, Turid Rugaas, Murray Sidman, and others who believe it's possible to train a dog—or raise a family, or live a successful life—using the principle of positive reinforcement instead of coercion or force.

Success Story

Last night, I graduated an in-home client from our seven-week basic course. He and his wife were constantly fighting about their year-old Basset hound's bad behavior and had called us as a last resort. The Basset was headed for the pound if we could not help.

They just could not believe the change in their dog's behavior as the weeks passed. I was amazed to see the lights come on in this dog's eyes as we taught it new lessons and tricks. The attention that the dog gave to the owners as they worked through the weeks just got better and stronger. After having the owners put the dog, Madison, through heel, sit, sit and stay, come from sit stay, down and stay, come from down stay, go to place, and come from place, I graduated the owners and dog from our basic clicker class.

I also taught the owners how to use clicker training to desensitize Madison so she could have her nails clipped, her ears cleaned, and be calm at the vet. Here is the real success story: The owners took Madison to the vet on Saturday because she was limping. Madison was clicked and treated for sitting quietly in the waiting room which she did even with other dogs acting up. According to her record, before the vet will look at her feet or ears they must put a soft muzzle on her because she was listed as an aggressive dog. The vet tech forgot, and the vet came in to see Madison. The owners started to click and treat Madison for lying calmly on the table, not reacting to the vet. Madison did great, and the vet was impressed. The vet, after examining Madison, opened her chart and could not believe this was the same dog they had seen before. The vet took the muzzle requirement out of Madison's file.

Clicker training saved Madison from the pound!

Lyle A. Reed, Roseville, CA

Will it work for my dog?

Within the world of traditional, compulsion-based training, a myth has arisen that certain breeds are not trainable. Or that certain dogs require "a firm hand." I hear it over and over: "But my dog is different!" You're right. Your dog is different. He's different from every other dog out there in any number of ways.

In the first place, different breeds were bred for entirely different things, and this means that each breed comes with its own set of training challenges. It's a lot easier to teach a Lab to retrieve than it is a Great Pyrenees. Teaching tracking to a bloodhound is piece of cake, but this task is a bit more challenging when you're dealing with a Chihuahua.

Some breeds were bred to work very closely with humans—herding breeds, some working breeds, sporting breeds. These dogs tend to excel at typical obedience behaviors. Others were bred to work completely independently or to do just one thing (and do it very, very well)—livestock guardian breeds, hounds, terriers. These dogs tend to be more difficult to train for obedience behaviors. A dog's breed, or combination of breeds, will be one of the factors that determines what the dog learns easily and what he will learn slowly, what she will do simply for the joy of doing it and what she will do only on the basis of "What's in it for me?"

Now add to the equation the unique characteristics of individual dogs and their past experiences. Any breeder will tell you that two dogs of the same breed can be as different as night and day. There are Newfies who hate the water, Labs who don't like to retrieve, and herding dogs who prefer the couch. There are hard dogs, soft dogs, fearful dogs, confident dogs, friendly dogs, and aloof dogs—and you can find individuals of each kind within a single breed!

What does this mean to the trainer? It means that smart trainers learn everything they can about dogs in general, about specific breeds, and most importantly, about a particular dog's history. This provides a background for identifying what the training challenges will be.

For example, a bloodhound is hard-coded to track. He wants to have his head down searching for scents *all* the time. In the competition obedience ring, however, you need your dog to focus on you. Where you can train attention easily in most breeds, this will likely be a challenge with a bloodhound, particularly in unfamiliar situations filled with unfamiliar scents. What's more, it will be a *constant* challenge. You are fighting instinct, and he will always have an innate desire to put his head down and sniff. So you will have to actively train "eyes up" until the day you retire him from the ring.

But it *can* be done. A challenge is just that. A challenge. Not an insurmountable obstacle. No dog is immune to the principles of learning. Barring a physical or psychological problem that prevents learning, your dog can be trained to do anything he or she is capable of doing—and clicker training is the tool you need to do it!

Clicker training is more than a cookbook method. It isn't as simple as click then treat. In some ways it's more difficult than traditional training because the onus is on you to teach, not on the dog to learn. You are responsible for motivating your dog, reading your dog's responses, and customizing every exercise to your dog's ability. But if you do this, if you learn the principles underlying the technology and master the mechanical skills, clicker training will work for your dog. Guaranteed.

Success Story

Eve is a chow/husky, not the kind of dog people think of when they think of obedience. She is dominant, independent, aloof. Basically, she's a dog who does things for herself, not for her human. I just wanted to have fun with her and make sure she was well mannered enough to take places so we could have more fun. On my other dog [mailing] lists, I kept hearing mention of something called "clicker training." I finally asked and someone explained the basics and told me about [ClickerSolutions]. I read and learned and bought some books and it all just clicked. "How cool!" I thought. This would work with my dog! And it has.

She isn't an obedience champion and she doesn't know many tricks, but she does everything I have taught her at the level I have taught. After all, we can't expect a dog to heel for fifty feet when she has not been taught to heel for fifty feet! But she will heel for several feet and automatically sit at heel. She has the best manners, both with humans and other dogs, of any dog I know. She enjoys her little tricks and enjoys performing. Most importantly, our bond has deepened to the point that I swear we can read each others' minds. Clicker training really has allowed me to truly look at my dog and how she responds to things. She is attentive and responsive and downright affectionate to me now. Her whole demeanor has become brighter when we train! Shining eyes; a high, wagging tail; smiling, wide open mouth— just the picture of a happy dog. She is still aloof with strangers but not with me. Not with me.

Anna Carolyn Abney, Greenwood, SC

I'm interested in canine sports.
Can a dog be clicker trained for activities such as agility, tracking, competition obedience, flyball, or Schutzhund?

Absolutely!

Recently I took an informal survey of trainers who subscribe to the ClickerSolutions mailing list. The result was a roster of clicker-trained dogs performing in the following sports, activities, and canine careers:

competition obedience

rally obedience

agility

conformation (stacking and gaiting)

herding

hunt tests

field work

tracking

search and rescue

flyball

canine freestyle

Schutzhund and other protection sports

canine frisbee

carting/draft

water rescue

service dog work

drug detection and other scent work

police work

guide dog work

therapy work

TV and film work

What's more, these dogs aren't just participating. They're excelling and winning! Clicker training enables you to train incredibly precise, incredibly reliable behaviors—perfect for performance animals.

see also

I don't simply want to participate—I want to win! Are clicker-trained behaviors precise enough and reliable enough for competition? **page 110**

You say I can do competition obedience, but I can't use a clicker or food in the ring. How can I clicker train? **page 111**

Where can I find a class or private trainer?

Clicker training is growing in popularity. Unfortunately, the number of people claiming to teach clicker training—but doing so incorrectly—is growing just as quickly.

There is no law that requires the certification of dog trainers or establishes standards by which someone is labeled a trainer—whatever methods he or she is using. I say I'm a trainer, so I am. What's more, at present there is no entity or organization that can enforce a universally agreed-upon definition of clicker training. There are "clicker trainers" out there who mix the use of clickers with physical "corrections," such as jerks on the collar or even electric shock.

I can't find a clicker class. **page 9**

see also

It is your responsibility to decide what methods you will and won't accept. Are you willing to accept a combination of clickers and corrections? Do you want to avoid corrections during training but find yourself more open-minded about using such *aversives* to stop problem behavior? Or do you want to avoid the use of aversives entirely?

When you visit a class or speak with a trainer, have a clear idea about what is and isn't acceptable. Don't compromise and don't be fooled by buzzwords. Lots of trainers have latched onto the phrases of "positive reinforcement" and "clicker training" but have, in essence, made absolutely no change to their correction-based way of training.

Once you identify a potential trainer, the real test is the trainer's ability to communicate with you and to teach you how to train your dog. The following tips will help you determine if a particular trainer is a good fit for you:

• Observe a class or a client session. If the trainer won't let you do that, look elsewhere.

• What methods are being taught and/or used during the session? If you don't feel comfortable with even one thing, this isn't the class for you.

• Are the students *and* their dogs happy and relaxed? Are they having fun? If not, keep looking.

Here are four potential sources of trainers. Note that even the online sources listing clicker trainers do not guarantee a given trainer is true to the clicker philosophy espoused in this book. No matter how you find a trainer, you must do your research and make sure this trainer is a good fit for you.

Clicker Teacher's List

http://www.travelvan.net/cgi-bin/marge/mainpage.pl

An online list compiled by Marge Morgan. A trainer is added to the list upon his or her request. Although the page defines clicker training as positive reinforcement training, any trainer can submit his or her name.

ClickerSolutions mailing list

http://groups.yahoo.com/group/ClickerSolutions

Although ClickerSolutions does not maintain a list of trainers, members are free to ask the list for recommendations.

The Association of Pet Dog Trainers (APDT)

http://www.apdt.com

1-800-PET-DOGS

The largest dog training association in the world, APDT was created to educate trainers about dog-friendly training methods. Although there are a large number of positive trainers in APDT, any trainer may join. Interview the trainer or observe a class to make certain a particular trainer is right for you. APDT's new trainer certification program promises to ensure a trainer well-grounded in learning theory.

National Association of Dog Obedience Instructors (NADOI)

http://www.nadoi.org

NADOI certification is highly coveted among dog trainers, but NADOI does not restrict itself to any particular method. Again, it's imperative for you to determine if the trainer is right for you.

- How does the trainer react when the student asks questions? Being open and willing to explain is a good sign; defensiveness or arrogance is not.

- If it's important to you to find a trainer who doesn't use aversives, ask very specific questions about how she defines aversives; when she feels aversives are necessary and which ones she would use in those circumstances; how she handles barking in class or other common problem situation. If you aren't comfortable with the answers, don't sign up.

- Finally, how do you get along with the trainer? Do you understand his explanations? After all, even if everyone else loves him, if you don't understand him, it's a waste of time and money. And, by all means, if you don't like him, look elsewhere!

After you choose a trainer, remember you're still the dog's owner. Don't turn over your dog's leash unless you know what the trainer is going to do. Don't let the trainer correct your dog. If at any point you feel uncomfortable, call it a lesson learned and leave—even if you've paid money for the class or session.

Don't let a bad experience with a trainer damage your relationship with your dog.

I can't find a clicker class.
Will it confuse my dog if I attend a class that uses another method?

If you don't have the opportunity to take a clicker class, you sometimes have to make do. The techniques used in non-clicker classes generally fall into two categories: lure-and-reward or traditional, compulsion-based.

Where can I find a class or a private trainer? **page 7**

see also

Lure-and-reward also relies on positive reinforcement, but instead of using a marker signal like the clicker to identify the correct behavior first, the primary reinforcer (food) is used to lead the dog through the behavior and then delivered at the moment the behavior occurs. Too often this lure is improperly faded, which results in the dog becoming more focused on the reward than its own behavior.

Traditional training methods frequently rely on training collars (chokes or prongs) to "correct" mistakes made by the dog. New behaviors are taught by physically guiding the dog through the behavior, and almost immediately, corrections are given for failing to perform the behavior. The dog learns to do the new behavior in order to avoid a correction. A drawback to this method is that corrections are dependent on physical control of the dog. Dogs often learn to perform behaviors only when wearing a training collar and leash.

The class you find may use a combination of these methods. Traditional classes may use food and lures, and lure-and-reward classes may sometimes use physical corrections. It is your responsibility to determine what is and isn't acceptable for you, but you may have the opportunity to use your clicker in a traditional or lure-and-reward class. If you do, keep the following tips in mind.

• First, discuss your plans with the instructor, and make sure it's okay to bring your clicker. Since you'll be "doing your own thing," you want to be certain you don't abuse the privilege.

• Try to be as unobtrusive as possible. Even though you're not using the instructor's methods, try to follow his or her class plan as much as possible.

- If people ask questions about what you're doing, answer honestly, but don't try to convince them to change methods. Offer your e-mail address or phone number if they want more information, or offer to discuss what you're doing in more depth after class.

- Don't say anything negative about the instructor, the methods, or any part of the class. It will reflect poorly on you and on clicker training, and it will make the instructor less open to what you are doing.

- Before class starts, speak to the instructor about corrections. If you're planning not to use any, say so. Make sure the instructor understands that you won't be squirting the dog for barking, collar popping for misbehaving, or forcing the dog to do an exercise the two of you haven't learned yet.

- Ask the instructor not to use your dog for demonstrations—simply explain that you're new at this and would prefer that no one else handle the dog. It's a common request.

- To lessen the stress on you and your dog, try to work a week ahead of everyone else. You want your dog to "know" the behaviors before each class, so you won't feel pressured to force her into performing a behavior she doesn't know. Begin by calling the instructor to ask what behaviors will be practiced in the very first class session.

- Teach attention, sit, and loose-leash walking prior to attending a traditional class because these behaviors are heavily emphasized. (How to use a clicker to train each of these behaviors is covered in Chapter 11, "Specific Behaviors.") Not only are these basic behaviors among the most useful, in the process of training for them you—and your dog—will learn how clicker training works.

Unfortunately, taking a clicker dog to a traditional class isn't always successful. Once you've switched to a positive, proactive way of training, it can be hard to watch others use reactive, punishment-based methods.

Final word: Your dog comes first. Do only what makes you feel good about learning together—don't risk your relationship for the sake of a class.

Since I started clicker training, if my dog or someone else's dog does something bad, I'll say, "Look—badly trained dog." Previously I would have said, "Look—*bad dog.*" I think it somehow causes us to move the responsibility from our dogs to ourselves, which then of course, gives you much more power to actually do something about it.

Dr. Tracie Barber, Sydney, Australia

CHAPTER 2 Equipment

What kind of equipment
do I need?

The only necessities for clicker training are an animal, a clicker or other marker signal, and treats or other reinforcer your animal will work for. Additionally, you might use a collar, a leash, a target or target stick, or a video camera.

The Clicker

A clicker is just a small tin noisemaker. A party favor. It has no inherent meaning to the dog. It has no magic powers. It's just a tool. The power of the clicker lies in its use as an event marker. (See Chapter 3, "The Magical Click.")

Clickers aren't the only event markers. Dolphin trainers use whistles, which are more easily heard under water. Trainers of deaf animals often use a brief flash of light. Some dog trainers prefer to use a verbal marker—either a sound or a word such as "Yes" or "Good."

To be most effective, the marker should be:

• unique

• consistent

• immediate

Although verbal markers have the advantage of being more readily available and of keeping your hands free, they're not as precise as a mechanical sound and aren't particularly unique. If you're training pet-quality behaviors, a verbal marker may or may not be sufficient. However, if you're a professional trainer or a serious hobbyist, a unique marker, like the clicker, will yield better results.

Treats and Other Positive Reinforcers

A positive reinforcer is anything your dog will work for in a given situation. Think about the last part of that statement. Anything *your dog*

see also

How do I juggle all the equipment? I need eight hands! **page 5**

Where can I get a clicker? **page 16**

What can I use to reinforce my dog? **page 28**

will work for *in a given situation*. That means that what reinforces one dog may not reinforce another, and what reinforces your dog in one situation may not work in another time and place.

In the living room, where there are virtually no distractions, your dog may willingly work for a few Cheerios. But in the backyard, with its mild distractions, you might have to use bits of cheese or roast chicken. And at a dog park, full of major distractions, food might not work at all! As a clicker trainer, part of your job is to discover what reinforcers will work for your dog in each specific situation.

Common reinforcers include food, toys, pats and praise, and even the opportunity to do something the dog wants to do. For example, you notice that the dog wants to go outside and play in the yard. At the door, you ask for a sit, and when he sits you open the door and let him out. Letting him do what *he* wanted has reinforced the sit that *you* wanted.

Collars, Leashes, and Other Restraints

Any plain collar or body harness will do for clicker training. In fact, often a collar isn't needed at all. In clicker training, a collar is used only to attach to a leash for safety purposes; it isn't used to control the dog or to deliver corrections.

Since you won't be giving collar corrections, don't use a slip (choke) collar or a pinch collar (one with prongs) in order to avoid giving accidental corrections that might inhibit your dog's willingness to experiment to figure out what might earn a click. If you have a greyhound or other breed that can slip out of a regular collar, use a limited slip or martingale. If your dog pulls on the leash, consider using a head halter until you train him to walk nicely. Body harnesses are wonderful but are ill-advised for persistent pullers.

For a clicker trainer, a leash is simply a tether to keep your dog safe when you're in an unfenced area or any other place where you need to keep the dog close at hand. Choose one that feels comfortable to you. Since you don't need it in your hands to deliver a correction, consider getting a leash long enough to tie around your waist. This will free your hands for other things.

Some trainers use different leashes in different situations:

• standard six-foot leather leash for brief walks,

• retractable lead[1] for longer walks,

• 20-foot (or longer) leash for working at a distance in unfenced areas.

Targets and Target Sticks

A target is an object a dog learns to touch with his nose, paw, or other body part. For example, service dogs are often taught to paw a particular target, which can then be placed anywhere in the environment to teach them to paw other objects, such as a cabinet door or a light switch. Because this kind of target is usually faded—gradually removed from the picture—it's best to use something that can be slowly decreased in size, such as a Post-It note, a piece of duct tape, or lid from a plastic container.

A target stick is a mobile target used as a lure to lead the dog from place to place. It can be as simple or elaborate as you want, from a specially made collapsible target stick to a piece of wooden doweling or an old TV antenna. Consider adding something with a contrasting color to the end of the stick for the dog to focus on, and make sure it's free of rough, jagged, or pointy edges.

Video Camera

A video camera is probably the most undervalued, overlooked, and vital piece of equipment available to trainers. During training, you must be cognizant of many things—your dog, your own performance, and triggers in the environment. Focusing on one thing often causes you to miss other things. Objective feedback, then, is vital. A video camera is the second-best thing to a personal coach. It provides a lasting record of your actual training, giving you the opportunity not only to review exactly what happened but also to compare performances over time.

---

[1] A retractable lead seems like a terrific choice: it's short when you need it to be short and long when you need it to be long. However, retractable leads require the dog to pull in order to extend the cord—exactly what you don't want your dog to do if you're training for walking on a loose leash. Also, for safety reasons, never use a retractable leash with a head halter.

How do I juggle all the equipment?
I need eight hands!

Keeping track of a dog, a leash, a clicker, treats, and a target stick seems like a job for an octopus. Using one or more of the following tips will make the task more manageable.

- Keep treats in a belt pouch or in a bowl (or series of bowls) instead of in your hands.

- Do initial training at home and in secure areas where you don't have to use a leash.

- When you need a leash, tie it around your waist, to a belt loop on your pants, or to a secure object so your hands will be free.

- If using a target stick, glue a clicker to the stick, so you can hold both clicker and stick in the same hand.

- Use the clicker for initial training only. Once the behavior is fully shaped, put on cue, and strong, you don't need the clicker to identify the desired behavior anymore. At that point, replace it with a release word. (See "When and how do I fade the clicker?" in Chapter 9.)

Practice, practice, practice. As Bob Bailey—a practitioner with decades of experience with many kinds of animals—is fond of saying, "Training is a mechanical skill." Unless you practice clicking and treating and working with the equipment, your performance will be awkward, and your dog's training may suffer from your own lack of precision.

see also

What kind of equipment do I need?
page 12

Is the timing of the click important?
page 44

Where can I get a clicker?

see also

Where I can I find a class or a private trainer? **page 12**

What kind of equipment do I need? **page 7**

Fortunately, clicker training is becoming more prevalent, but clickers themselves are still notoriously difficult to find in some places.

PETsMART has begun carrying them, and PetCo carries clickers bundled with some books. Clicker trainers often sell them as well. The easiest place to find clickers is on the Internet. Try these sites:

www.clickertraining.com
Karen Pryor's Clicker Training™. Books, videos, resources, and a wide range of information about clicker training by Karen Pryor and other leading clicker trainers are available at www.clickertraining.com. The company also offers introductory kits for new clicker trainers.

www.dogwise.com
Dogwise offers a wide variety of current books and products for serious dog enthusiasts and trainers through their web site and at dog shows across the country.

CHAPTER 3 That Magical Click

What does the click mean?

see also

Does the click have to be followed by a food treat? **page 21**

Does the click have to end the behavior? **page 20**

What is "charging the clicker," and how do I do it? **page 42**

The click should always mean the same thing. Always. Every time. Period.

As trainer, you decide what the click means. For most trainers, the click means the following things:

• That behavior is something I like.

• You've earned a reinforcer.

• The behavior is over.

That's the definition I use, and the one I recommend. However, some trainers do not want the click to signal an end to the behavior (to mean the dog can get up from a stay, for example). That's fine, as long as they are consistent in that definition from the beginning. It's changing the click's meaning arbitrarily that makes the dog's job unnecessarily harder.

Does the click have to end the behavior?

see also

What is a keep-going signal? **page 188**

No. As the trainer, you define what the click means.

But once you decide, stick with your definition. The click should mean the same thing every time, in every situation. Most trainers do define the click as the end of the behavior.

Do I have to treat after every click?

Yes! Eventually the clicker will be replaced by a release word and you may choose at that point to reinforce on a more variable schedule. But when using the clicker, each click is followed by a treat.

You don't have to use food, but during training every click should be followed by something the dog wants—something the dog is willing to work for.

The click is powerful because the dog learns it means she's going to get something she really wants. In a way, the click is like money. When we humans do our jobs we get money, and we use that money to get what we really want—food, clothing, shelter, entertainment. The dog earns a click, and then receives a reinforcer she really wants.

On the old TV show "Gilligan's Island," one of the running jokes was Mr. Howell's continued attempts to "buy" things from other characters with boxes of cash. Of course cash, though supremely important in civilization, had no value whatsoever on the island—there was nothing there that the others needed money to buy! Without the "what we really want" to back it up, cash is just pretty paper.

The click is no different. It's powerful only as long as it's followed by something the dog wants—consistently and, since you're marking a behavior as it happens, immediately.

Some trainers will say it's fine to click without a treat sometimes—and I've heard others recommend doing so in order to frustrate the dog into doing something different. (If you want to elicit new behaviors, though, you can get the same response by simply withholding the click!)

Some trainers even believe that once the click is conditioned, you have to follow it with a treat or other primary reinforcer only occasionally. But there are dangers in taking such an approach.

see also

Does the click have to be followed by a food treat? **page 21**

Will I have to use the clicker and treats forever? **page 23**

What can I use to reinforce my dog? **page 28**

My dog isn't interested in food/is on a restricted diet/is overweight. Can I still clicker train? **page 32**

Does the reward have to follow the click immediately? **page 34**

How do I move from food treats to praise only? **page 37**

When and how do I fade the clicker? **page 97**

- While some dogs will "work for the click" alone, others will not, and if the dog doesn't respond, the trainer may blame the technology, not his execution.

- Or, alternatively, the trainer may blame the animal—the dog is labeled "stubborn," "dominant," "stupid," "hardheaded," or (my favorite) "bored."

- The trainer may have success to a certain point, and then not understand that working for the click alone is not enough—for example, in an environment full of distractions. Again, the trainer is then likely to blame either the animal or the technology for the failure, not his execution.

Obviously, it is *possible* not to treat after every click, but considering the click's importance as an event marker, why would you want to risk weakening the power of the click in any way? In my view, for good trainers a click *always* equals reinforcement.

Note: Occasionally a dog will refuse an offered reinforcement while working. This does not mean you should stop reinforcing after the click. If your dog refuses your treat, reconsider what you're offering. Your dog is likely telling you there's something he wants more. Use it!

Does the click have to be followed by a food treat?

Food is an excellent reinforcer—one of the most powerful you have.

- It's a primary reinforcer, something your dog naturally needs to survive.

- Different foods have different "values" to the dog. You can use a lower value food in a low-distraction environment and a higher value food for a high-distraction situation.

- There's a limitless variety of food, and mixing a variety of low, medium, and high value foods will help keep your dog interested.

- Food can be cut into tiny bites that are easy to deliver and quickly eaten, enabling you to do a lot of repetitions in a single training session.

For all of these reasons, I prefer to pair the click with a food treat at the start. Once a behavior is on cue and strong, I simultaneously replace the sound of the clicker with a release word and phase in alternative reinforcers. Eventually, I use alternative reinforcers—primarily the opportunity to do something the dog wants—almost exclusively. But in the beginning, when I'm working on a new behavior, I rely on food entirely.

Ultimately, though, the reward doesn't have to be a food treat. It can be anything your dog is willing to work for in that particular situation. Remember, if your dog won't actively work for what you're offering—food or otherwise—it isn't a reinforcer in that situation.

see also

Do I have to treat after every click? **page 19**

What can I use to reinforce my dog? **page 28**

My dog isn't interested in food/is on a restricted diet/is overweight. Can I still clicker train? **page 32**

What if I can't offer a food treat or if my dog isn't interested in the reward I'm offering? **page 33**

All these treats…aren't I spoiling my dog? **page 36**

How do I move from food treats to praise only? **page 37**

My dog doesn't seem to know
the clicker means anything except that a treat is coming. How can I teach her that the click is an event marker?

All dogs take a while to learn that the clicker is more than a treat announcer. This means consistency and good timing on your part, plus experience and time.

see also

How do I begin shaping? **page 84**

The best way to get this connection is by capturing and shaping a behavior the dog does spontaneously. Luring is a fast way to get behavior—you entice a dog to do something, then click and treat. But if you want your dog to learn to rely on the click as a source of information, then the click needs to be the primary way she figures out what to do.

A clicker-savvy dog—one who has figured out that the clicker is an event marker—will experiment to find out exactly what is making you click. Other dogs may merely repeat what's worked in the past. Guess what. It doesn't matter. All that matters is the rate of emitted behavior. Rather than trying to determine what your dog has or hasn't figured out, keep some basic records. Then you'll have data to tell you if you're getting the response you want and how reliable that response is.

Success Story

After I got my first clicker, I ran home to do "101 Things to Do with a Box." I got nothing from my dog. She stared at me, lay down, walked off. Poor dog. She didn't know what I wanted. She'd never seen me like that: eyes glued to her, holding my breath, acting insane.

Finally, I gave up and tried to teach her to touch my hand instead. She caught on immediately. Because it's so easy to teach, you run less of a risk of acting strangely around your dog and inhibiting her. Now touch is her favorite thing to do.

I have her touch my hand several times every day before I give her a treat ball. She leaps around, being very dramatic and excited about touching my hand. When I used to just hand her the treat ball, or make her sit first, she was never excited about getting it. Now she's ecstatic.

Now I use the clicker for everything. I can't imagine how I'd train without it. The look on her face as she's running to me after the click is priceless.

Erica Nance, New York City, NY

Should I carry the clicker around
and click and treat every time I see the dog doing something I like?

What's your goal? A well-mannered pet? Or more precise behaviors from a competition or working dog?

If your dog is a pet and only a pet, feel free to click and treat whenever you see your dog doing something you like. The click is a very clear signal to the dog that he's doing something right!

If your dog is destined to be a competition or working dog you want the clicker to be as powerful as it can possibly be. Since its power lies in its use as an event marker, not a treat marker, make sure it remains an event marker by using it in training situations where your dog can experiment to find out exactly what behavior you're marking, or in new circumstances when you want to inform the dog that he's making a good move or decision.

In either case, if you catch your dog doing something good outside of a formal training session, feel free to reward with a word or a mouth click and then a primary reinforcer.

> Anytime you have the opportunity to work with a clicker-savvy dog, do it! Dogs that are clicker trained and clicker savvy will teach you more in one session than you can learn from reading ten books.
>
> Michele Stone , La Jolla, CA

Will I have to use the clicker and treats forever?

see also

What can I use to reinforce my dog? **page 28**

How do I move from food treats to praise only? **page 37**

When and how do I fade the clicker? **page 97**

You say I can do competition obedience, but I can't use a clicker or food in the ring. How can I clicker train? **page 111**

The clicker is used to identify the behavior you like when the dog is learning. Once you've trained the behavior, you no longer need to mark it with the clicker.

As for treats, it's a bit more complicated. Just like you expect to be paid for going to work each week, so your dog expects (and deserves) to be paid for doing what you ask.

I believe it was trainer Gary Wilkes who originated the bank account analogy. Reinforcing behavior is like adding money to a bank account. The bigger the balance, the more likely the dog will do the behavior when you ask for it—and the more interest you earn! If you ignore a behavior, you make a withdrawal. If you punish it, you make a big withdrawal. If you stop making deposits (by reinforcing the behavior) and start making withdrawals (through lack of reinforcement), eventually the bank account will run dry, and you'll lose the behavior.

Don't take desired behavior for granted. You don't have to reinforce it with food treats forever—but boy, it's special when you do! Other times praise and a pat are plenty.

My dog is afraid of the clicker!
What do I do?

Honestly, this isn't an unusual problem. A clicker makes a very sharp sound, one that works so well in part, it is believed, because it stimulates a primitive, emotional, instinctive part of the brain called the amygdala.

To make the sound less startling, at first, you can layer the metal tab of the clicker with medical adhesive tape—each strip will make it quieter. Then, as the dog becomes less reactive to the noise, you can begin peeling off the tape one strip at a time. You can further muffle the sound by holding it in your pocket.

Alternatively, you can use the "button" on a drink bottle or baby food jar lid or even the button on a ballpoint pen.

You may find that any mechanical click sound scares your dog at first. In that case, do the following things:

- Switch to a mouth click, a sound made with your tongue and cheek, temporarily.

- Wear the clicker around your neck all the time, so the dog gets used to seeing it.

- Click once before you set down his dinner to build an association between the sound and something he really wants.

Be very nonchalant about these steps. Ignore any fearful behavior. Remain upbeat and go on about your business like everything is normal. Most of all, be patient. Wait until your dog alerts—but doesn't startle—at the sound of the clicker before using it for training.

see also

What kind of equipment do I need?
page 12

How do I handle fearful behavior?
page156

Success Story

I'll never forget when I first got started. I'd adopted this adorable Jack Russell terrier from the Animal Rescue Foundation, who informed me she'd been adopted and returned twice. She was so darned cute I took her anyway, certain any dog could be trained. In looking for an obedience school, I noticed a "new" kind of training—clicker training—and it caught my fancy. So I researched clicker training, bought books, a clicker, a target stick, and contacted a local trainer, enrolled in classes. Unfortunately, the classes didn't start for a few months. But it looked easy, so I thought I'd be ahead of the game when the classes started.

Armed with treats, clicker and a book, I coaxed my little urchin into the kitchen, clicked, and OOPS—she ran for dear life, [hid] under the coffee table and wouldn't come out until I put the clicker away, got down on my hands and knees with a big piece of chicken, and bribed her out. Certain I'd made a mistake, I called the trainer and told her what had just occurred. "First," she said, laughing, "you clicked right in the dog's ear. That's enough to scare anyone under the coffee table." Then she proceeded to tell me some dogs are afraid of the noise of the clicker in the beginning. "Put some adhesive tape over the clicker, your hand and clicker in your pocket or behind your back and start over." She said this would mute the sound so Scruffy wouldn't be so startled.

Needless to say, it worked beautifully. Within a week, my little ruffian was sitting on cue, looking forward to her training sessions. It took about two weeks before I could remove the adhesive tape—and I never again clicked right in her ear. That was my first pearl of wisdom.

Jan Niemeyer, Bixby, OK

CHAPTER 4 Reinforcement

What can I use to reinforce my dog?

Anything your dog wants!

You have a variety of reinforcers available. Some of the most commonly used include:

- food
- toys
- praise or attention
- the opportunity to do something the dog wants to do
- the opportunity to perform a well-known behavior

In a formal training session you want to get as many repetitions as possible. Food is an excellent reinforcer because it can be cut into tiny pieces that the dog can eat quickly. Toys are also good reinforcers, but playing with the toy takes time, meaning you get fewer repetitions in a session. Praise and attention are wonderful additions to food or toys but may not be desirable enough, from the dog's point of view, to use alone, particularly in distracting situations.

Giving your dog the opportunity to do something he wants to do can be a most powerful reinforcer when circumstances permit. For virtually all dogs, interacting with the natural environment—greeting another dog, chasing a squirrel, or just getting to go outside and play—is innately reinforcing.

In addition to letting your dog do something he wants to do—like greeting a visitor—you can also use previously learned behaviors as reinforcement. In fact, the reinforcing nature of performing a well-known behavior is one of the reasons why back chaining—a technique for training an animal to do a series of actions in response to a single cue by first teaching the behaviors in reverse order—works so well.

No matter what reinforcer you choose, consider its relative value. One food might be worth more than another food. Your dog's tug toy might be worth more to your dog than food in one situation. In another, the opportunity to greet another dog may be the best treat of all! It all depends on your dog and the particular situation.

Just remember, when picking your reinforcer the *dog* determines what's reinforcing. You may want to use kibble, but if your dog wants roast chicken, roast chicken will get better results.

> Food isn't always the best reward. Use whatever is a reward at the time. At the park, a tennis ball is the only thing that will get Arden's attention. If she lies down, we throw the ball. I first got attention at the park by teaching her that she got to run around only after she had given me her paw. It took ages the first time, but she worked it out very quickly after that.
>
> Dr. Tracie Barber, Sydney, Australia

Shouldn't my dog be working for me
or for the love of the job instead of for food?

Traditional trainers use this argument a lot. However, if a dog chooses not to do what they ask, they "correct" it—that is, they inflict a punishment such as a jerk on the dog's collar. The dog quickly learns that not doing what the trainer asks causes bad things to happen. Once corrections enter the picture, how can anyone be sure whether the dog is working for the trainer—or to avoid a correction?

Internal motivation is a wonderful thing—a desire to excel, to succeed. Unfortunately, you can't depend on an animal's having the internal motivation to do what you want it to do.

Many breeds of dogs were bred to do specialized jobs. Those dogs have an internal drive to perform those tasks. It's unlikely you'd have to use external reinforcement to train a border collie to herd sheep, a bloodhound to track, or an Afghan hound to lure course. However when we add human-defined restrictions to these behaviors—for example, teaching a bloodhound to track a particular scent—positive reinforcement is the best way to communicate which aspect of the behavior we're trying to encourage.

Most of the behaviors we ask dogs to do are arbitrary human-defined behaviors that have no meaning to the dog. Your puppy is probably completely neutral toward sitting down when you start training it. But by externally reinforcing your dog for sitting, you are associating the behavior with good things. Through classical conditioning, then, the behavior itself takes on a positive emotional association. Your dog may receive internal reinforcement for performing the behavior when cued. More importantly, you become a "giver of good things," giving you a positive emotional association.

Does it happen every time? No, because positive reinforcement is not the only force in play. For example, if you routinely crate your dog after calling it—and the dog doesn't like being crated—then the recall itself can take on a negative association. Other factors include:

• the dog's emotional state

• its health

• its genetic propensity for trainability or for performing a given behavior

• stress in the environment

• your attitude toward training and that behavior

• significant events that occur during training

• the pleasantness or unpleasantness of whatever routinely follows this behavior

• physical comfort or discomfort associated with the behavior

• the "fun factor"

It's the sum total of all of these factors over time that determines whether an individual dog will develop a positive or negative association toward doing a particular behavior—or toward "working" in general.

A good trainer will endeavor to control as many of those factors as possible, so the sum total equals a positive experience. A happy dog is happy because of what you do. Why threaten the positive association by removing the external reinforcement?

My dog isn't interested in food
is on a restricted diet/is overweight. Can I still clicker train?

Yes, you can.

Although you can use alternative reinforcers, food is still one of the easiest to use in a training session because it's small, quick to deliver, and powerful. You'll find it easier to maintain a high rate of reinforcement than with other treats.

Here are some tips for using food as a reinforcer:

- Use the smallest treat you can. How small? Cheerio-size or smaller. You want to give your dog a taste, not fill him up.

- Train when your dog is hungry—before, rather than after, a meal.

- If your dog is on a restricted diet, use small pieces of his regular food as training treats. However, be aware it's not likely to be a very powerful reinforcer, particularly in distracting situations.

- If your dog is overweight or so small that he fills up easily, dole out his daily ration one piece at a time, feeding him what's left as a meal at the end of the day.

see also

Do I have to treat after every click? **page 19**

Does the click have to be followed by a food treat? **page 21**

What can I use to reinforce my dog? **page 28**

Tips for Treating Hard-to-Treat Dogs

For the short guys: treat them using a long-handled wooden kitchen spoon with sticky stuff smeared on it, such as peanut butter, strained baby food, or cream cheese.

For the pudgy guys: treat with cheerios and puffed rice flavored by being stored with nuked hot dogs or other stinky stuff. If you use kibble, reduce their meals by the same amount. Train active, calorie-burning tricks and obedience behaviors—such as heel, spin, or puppy pushups—instead of stay.

Erica Nance, New York City, NY

For a small dog on a heavy training day, place kibble in a bag mixed up with whatever treats you use—and remember to decrease the amount of kibble by the amount of treats. To make the kibble more like treats, try frying up some bacon. Then toss the kibble into the bacon fat and let it soak it up.

For dogs with weight problems, build toy drive by pairing the toy with favorite treats, by clicking and treating for interaction with the toy, and by making the toy a scarce resource that you jealously guard and have great fun with on your own. This makes for a treat that not only doesn't add calories, but actually uses them up!

Susan Mann, Wilmington, DE

What if I can't offer a food treat
or if my dog isn't interested in the reward I'm offering?

A reinforcer is anything your dog is willing to work for in a given situation. As trainer, it's your job to figure out what you can offer that your dog wants in any situation. Then you can:

• use what the dog wants as a reward

• provide something the dog wants more as a reward

• increase the perceived value of the reward you want to use

Complications arise when you want to provide one reinforcer but the dog wants something else that's present in the environment even more. If this happens, either change your training plan or change the environment.

Let's say, for example, that you're using your best roast chicken but your dog is more interested in passing dogs, bicycles, birds, children, joggers, etc. You can either use the opportunity to interact with the object of interest as a reinforcer or move further away from these distractions so that the reward you prefer to use becomes more important.

Another problem arises when you're restricted in what reinforcers you're allowed to use. For example, in an obedience competition, you can't bring food or toys into the ring, and obviously letting your dog interact with the judge or the cute dog in the next ring would be a really bad idea.

So what do you do? Figure out in advance what reinforcers you are going to use in the ring and increase their perceived value for your dog.

Between exercises in the obedience ring, you can praise your dog, give her pats or scritchies, celebrate with her, or ask her to perform favorite behaviors. Identify which of these behavioral reinforcers your dog enjoys the most, and choose one or more to do between exercises. Once you've decided, increase the value of these reinforcers. How? Pair them with primary reinforcers or activities your dog finds pleasurable.

see also

What can I use to reinforce my dog?
page 28

All these treats... aren't I spoiling my dog? **page 36**

How do I move from food treats to praise only? **page 37**

How do I train against distractions? **page 101**

You say I can do competition obedience, but I can't use a clicker or food in the ring. How can I clicker train? **page 111**

How can I get my dog to pay attention to me even in a distracting environment? **page 120**

What's the Premack principle? **page 190**

For example, pick a behavior and ask her to do it every day just before dinner. Wow! What a powerful reinforcer you're pairing it with! Is your dog reinforced by laughter? Train a funny trick and take it on the road. If it earns laughter every time the two of you perform it, she'll enjoy doing it. Are there certain behaviors your dog just seems to love to do for their own sake? Some dogs love to target. Some dogs love to spin. Ask for those behaviors just before you give a jackpot—a really big treat. Do the same thing with praise, scritchies, and celebrations—pair them consistently with jackpots and other favorite things.

After you've increased the value of these alternative reinforcers, phase them into your regular training routine.

Does the reward have to follow the click immediately?

The clicker is sometimes called a "bridging stimulus" because it bridges the time between the behavior and the primary reinforcer. Ideally, the reward should follow as soon as possible, but a few seconds' delay is usually acceptable.

However, although you may have defined the click as the end of the behavior, the dog has not. If he manages to slip in another behavior every time between the click and the treat (stands up right away after a sit, for instance), the dog will naturally chain that behavior onto the one you're training for.

To avoid that problem, tighten up your timing and make sure not to reinforce any pattern or regularity in behavior that occurs between the click and the treat.

If the click ends the behavior,
does it matter what the dog is doing when I deliver the reward?

Yes! The click is the event marker. That's true. But the reward that follows is still the primary reinforcer, and it will still reinforce the behavior the dog is doing when it is delivered.

Although a gap between the click and the treat can be a source of problems, you can also use it to your advantage. For example, in the "Be a Tree" method of teaching a dog not to pull on the leash, when the dog goes to the end of the leash, you would initially click at the moment the leash gets slack. Even though you click when the leash goes slack, deliver the treat in heel position. Take advantage of the reinforcing property of the primary reward, by reinforcing the dog for being in correct position.

Can I treat
without clicking?

Sure. If you miss an opportunity to click, don't weaken the clicker by clicking late. Just deliver the primary reinforcer.

Outside of a training session, feel free to reinforce desirable behavior anytime and every time it occurs, even if you don't have a clicker (or food treats) with you. Don't take good behavior for granted just because you don't have a clicker available.

One of the secrets to changing and shaping behavior is maintaining a high rate of reinforcement. When your dog is doing things you like, let the praise and treats flow freely!

All these treats...
am I spoiling my dog?

Spoiling occurs when you give something for nothing. Grandparents often lavish presents and treats on their grandchildren to show their love and affection—not because the children did something good; but only if the children began to demand those "freebies" as something due to them, would I consider them to be "spoiled."

In clicker training, you aren't spoiling your dog because you're not giving anything for free: you are very intentionally reinforcing desired behavior in order to make that behavior occur more frequently.

Indeed, your dog may offer those behaviors in order to "beg" for treats—but there are worse problems to have than a dog who continuously offers "good" behaviors. You certainly don't have to reinforce every offered behavior. If your dog is making a pest of herself by repeating her latest trick over and over, ignore her and stick to reinforcing that behavior only when you ask for it. However, if she offers a quiet sit instead of jumping on a visitor, make that behavior more likely to happen in the future by reinforcing it right away.

How do I move from food treats to praise only?

This question is often asked by pet owners or crossover trainers who are wary of being overly reliant on food in training and by competition obedience trainers who know they can't use food in the ring.

I reply to each the same way: if your dog does the work, he deserves a paycheck. Praise can be an effective reinforcer, but most dogs are unwilling to work for praise alone. This means that if you want to maintain the strength of the behavior you must continue to reward it, even if you're training for competition.

Patty Ruzzo, an extremely successful competition trainer, is often asked about "fading"—phasing out—food treats before competition. She says, "If you knew a famine was coming, would you starve your children to prepare them for it?" Of course not! You'd feed them!

The only time you can't reinforce your dog with food is during the trial performance itself. Think how many times you practice the required behaviors ahead of time. Actual performance is a small percentage of that total. Why deprive yourself of one the most powerful—not to mention incredibly convenient—reinforcers available to you during training?

All that said, you do need to phase in alternative reinforcers at some point, so the dog won't go into total shock in the ring. And if you're a pet owner, you'll sometimes need to use alternative rewards so your dog will remain happy and willing even when you don't have food available.

As noted earlier in this chapter, you have a whole slew of reinforcers available to you. Once you've chosen your alternative rewards it's time to phase them in like any other criteria—starting slow and building gradually over time. Here's a series of steps you might use:

• Do ten repetitions, or "reps," reinforcing with food after each one.

What can I use to reinforce my dog? **page 28**

What if I can't offer a food treat or if my dog isn't interested in the reward I'm offering? **page 33**

You say I can do competition obedience, but I can't use a clicker or food in the ring. How can I clicker train? **page 111**

see also

- Do ten reps. Reinforce with food after nine of them, with an alternative reinforcer after one. (Which one? Randomize. Number ten slips of paper, put them in a hat, mix them up, and draw one to determine which rep you'll reward with the alternative reinforcer. For example, you draw number three, so you do two reps with food, then use the alternative reinforcer on the next one, then reinforce with food for the remainder of the session.)

- Do ten reps, reinforcing with food after eight of them, with an alternative reinforcer for two. Randomize to determine which two.

- Do ten reps. Reinforce with food for seven and use an alternative reinforcer for the other three.

And so on. If you've properly conditioned your alternative reinforcers, there should be no lessening of attitude, since you're still using a reward of value. If there is a change in attitude, go back to basics and try to increase the value of your reinforcer more gradually.

One final word: Just because your dog now understands that the behavior may not be followed by a food treat doesn't mean you should cut out food treats entirely. Think of training along a bell curve; for every time you train without food, you should have a session using food only, and most sessions should fall somewhere in the middle—sometimes a few more food rewards, sometimes a few more alternative rewards. Be unpredictable!

Food for Thought

After reading about clicker training, I was expecting my dog to "get it" almost immediately. It helped me when I realized that not all dogs learn at the same rate. It was okay for her to take a couple weeks to learn, as long as she and I are still having fun….

One major thing I've learned is how much taking notes can help. When I'm forced to look at the details of each training session and think before going on to the next one, it greatly increases the chance my dog will be successful, and then I am successful. Success for me is being able to see clearly where the training is going and where mistakes may be made.

Ellen Ryan, Mobile, AL

How soon should I begin doing "two-fers" and "three-fers"?

A "two-fer" means a dog has to perform two behaviors in order to earn one click and one treat. Two sits, two downs, or a down and a sit. A "three-fer" is three behaviors for one click.

Many trainers add two-fers and three-fers during training as a way to phase out reliance on the clicker and treats or as the first step to a variable schedule of reinforcement (VSR). Variable reinforcement, also known as intermittent reinforcement, works on what's popularly called the slot-machine principle: as anyone who's visited a casino knows, just knowing you might get reinforced can be powerful motivation. But using two-fers, three-fers, and VSRs requires an understanding of what they are and how they may affect training.

What are your training goals for your dog? Are you looking for a well-mannered pet? Or are you training for a competitive sport?

For a pet dog, the cue "sit" means simply to put his rear end on the ground. Sometimes the sits are straight, sometimes not; sometimes they're neat and square; sometimes they're cockeyed. It really doesn't matter. Precision is not a requirement of the behavior. When the behavior is strongly on cue and the clicker has been replaced with a release word, that's the time to begin two-fers and three-fers and eventually a VSR, if the behavior requires it. If you do this too soon, however, your dog may become frustrated rather than intrigued, and so might quit trying. Properly added, a VSR will motivate the dog to try harder and make the behavior stronger, but it also encourages variable behavior. (Think of a gambler trying different "lucky" charms that don't, in fact, have any influence on the odds of winning.)

By contrast, a competition-quality sit is precise. For these dogs a sit must be tucked, straight, square, and fast. To get that precision, trainers shape one element at a time. To get a tucked sit, they click only tucked sits; if they don't click, that's a signal the dog has done something wrong and should try something different.

see also

How do I shape a complex behavior, such as a fast, straight, square sit?
page 88

Continuous reinforcement, differential reinforcement, variable reinforcement—what do these terms mean? And how are they relevant to my training?
page 186

Uh-oh. Bad news if you've been using two-fers, three-fers, and VSRs. A properly used VSR will create a stronger behavior—the animal will try harder and harder to earn reinforcement—but it will likely also cause variations in the behavior, which can then be a nuisance to undo.

Bottom line: Training is tough enough when you keep it as simple as possible. Two-fers and three-fers aren't necessary for achieving a strong, reliable behavior, they are potentially detrimental to precise behaviors, and they add an unnecessary level of complexity to your training. I'd advise you to make training as easy as possible on yourself and your dog: stick to continuous reinforcement.

CHAPTER 5 Getting Started

What is "charging the clicker," and how do I do it?

see also

My dog is afraid of the clicker! What do I do? **page 24**

Money is just paper, but because it's associated with the food, shelter, clothing, and entertainment it can purchase, that paper has great value to us humans. The clicker is like money to our dogs in that it stands for treats and other things the dog wants.

When you first introduce the clicker, it's just a plastic noisemaker. To make its sound valuable—to make the dog want to work for it—you have to associate it with food or another desired reinforcer. This process is called "charging the clicker."

Charging the clicker is easy. Click and immediately follow with a favorite treat. It should take only a few repetitions before the dog visibly alerts and looks for his treat when you click. However, you don't have to waste those first repetitions clicking for nothing; you can start training your dog right away by clicking for a desired behavior, such as eye contact (attention) or a sit.

Some dogs are frightened by the click sound at first. To help prevent this problem, at first put the clicker in your pocket when you click, in order to muffle the sound. Once the click has taken on a positive association, you can take it out of your pocket.

Success Story

Before we got Vincent, I knew next to nothing about German shepherds and very little about dog training. I read a bit about German shepherds on the Internet, and a lot of it dealt with how you need to show the dog, in no uncertain terms, that you are the "alpha." Not being an alpha kind of person, I began to think that I would probably never be able to handle a German shepherd. Then we met Vincent, in need of a new home, completely untrained, and the happiest, sweetest, most playful, wild-child, I-love-life dog I have ever seen. We fell in love instantly and brought him home.

By then, I had also come across clicker training on the Internet and it sounded like just the thing for someone not very alpha. It made a lot of sense to me to be able to focus on communication instead of domination. I bought some books and a clicker, got some treats, and started with "101 Things to Do with a Box." Vincent looked at the box. Click. Treat. Vincent looked at me and waited. And waited. And waited.

I decided to put the box away and work on attention instead. Vincent looked at me. Click. Treat. Vincent looked at me again. Click. Treat. Vincent went to check on the cat. Hmmm…

After going through this routine for a couple of days, I realized our communication was not what it should be, so I read some more about clicker training and the light bulb started to glow just a little. Could it be that his kibble isn't rewarding enough right after breakfast? Maybe the way I stare at him, trying to hypnotize him into touching the box, even leaning over him a little, makes him want to go do something else?

Later that evening we had just had dinner, and Vincent was very interested to know if there was anything left on our plates. I got the crazy idea to teach him to play the piano, just for fun. I started to click and treat whenever he got close to the piano. The treat was a small piece of anything from our plates, and boy did he get the idea fast this time! In ten minutes he was playing the piano with his nose. Big jackpot!

That was all I had intended to teach him, but Vincent had other plans—there was still food on those plates! Suddenly he stood on his back paws and put both his front paws on the piano, turning his head back at me at the same time, looking so much like a concert pianist that we laughed out loud.

Eva Thollander, Stockholm, Sweden

Is the timing of the click important?
How can I improve my timing?

see also

When should I click? (How do I choose my criteria?) **page 79**

I set my criteria, but my dog advanced a lot further than that. Should I raise my criteria accordingly? **page 82**

Timing, timing, timing. What's all the fuss about timing?

Timing is incredibly important. It's your timing of the click that transforms the clicker from a simple treat announcer into a precise, powerful *event* marker.

Ninety-five percent of training problems can be traced to three basic trainer errors:

- poor timing

- faulty criteria

- low rate of reinforcement

Set yourself and your dog up to succeed. Practice your timing.

Ideally, the click should happen at *exactly* the moment the behavior occurs—not even a fraction of a second early or late. Will your dog learn if your timing isn't that precise? Usually. Dogs, unlike some other species, are generally interested enough in the game to try to work out what you want them to do. However, the better your timing, the faster your training will go.

Timing is a skill. Perfect timing is obtained *only* through practice, and it's best to begin by practicing without the dog, when you can concentrate totally on timing. Included below are practices exercises for both one and two people. For best results, either video tape your practice or, even better, have someone watching who can tell you when you're early, late, or spot on.

- *Exercise #1:* This exercise is recommended by veteran animal trainer Bob Bailey. Have someone drop a ball from varying heights. Click at the moment the ball hits the ground. Your click and the sound of the ball's impact should occur simultaneously. The less distance the ball has to fall, the harder the exercise. If the ball is held just an inch off a table, for example, you'll have to hone your observation skills to figure out what happens just before your partner releases the ball.

The goal is not for your partner to trick you. The goal is for you to learn to see the tiny responses leading to a behavior. This is what you have to learn in order to have excellent timing when training.

- *Exercise #2:* Canadian clicker trainer Sue Ailsby taught me this one. Sit facing your partner. Click your partner's blinks. Count your clicks and have your partner count his blinks. After thirty seconds or a minute, stop and compare your counts.

- *Exercise #3:* Similar to Exercise #2. Have your partner touch your arm while you click the touches. The clicks and the touches should coincide perfectly.

- *Exercise #4:* If you're alone, use your TV to your advantage. Watch your favorite show and practice clicking scene changes. Or click your favorite actor every time he takes a drink, runs his hand through his hair, touches another person, or performs some other common behavior.

- *Exercise #5:* Take your clicker to work, to the mall, or to another public place. Pick a person, pick a behavior, and then click whenever the person does the behavior. Pick something simple, like foot or hand movements. (Do this with your clicker in your pocket to avoid drawing attention to yourself.)

My dog is too food-obsessed
to do anything but stare at the clicker and treats. What do I do?

see also

What can I use to reinforce my dog?
page 28

When and how do I fade the clicker?
page 47

How can I get my dog to pay attention to me even in a distracting environment?
page 120

First of all, be *thrilled* that you have a food-crazy dog. Training is a great deal easier with a dog who is eager to work for food treats.

You simply need to teach your dog to concentrate on you, even when food is present. This is the first step of attention training, which also includes proofing against other distractions. Food is a marvelous training tool. Dogs are born needing and wanting it—it's a natural reinforcer. But, like any tool, it must be used properly.

Teach Self-control to the Obsessed

Some dogs, often those who are unaccustomed to a lot of variety in their diet, become a bit too food-focused. A couple of basic attention exercises will help these dogs get their minds off the food and back on the task at hand.

Start by holding a piece of food in your closed fist. Your dog will probably sniff, lick, and paw at your fist to get you to open it. Instead, wait for the moment when the dog pauses in his exploration, then click and offer him the treat. Repeat until the dog learns that mugging your hand will get him nowhere and that holding back will earn a click and a treat.

Then raise your criteria. Hold the food away from you and wait until the dog looks up at your face. Just a glance—a flick of the eyes—is enough. Click and treat. Gradually increase your criteria until the dog maintains eye contact with you instead of staring at the treat hand.

Be patient. Don't call your dog's name—wait for him to offer the behavior. No matter how persistent he is, he has to take his eyes off the food at some point.

Keep the Treats Off Your Body

When you're training in the house, keep the treats in a bowl separate from you. It's okay if you have to walk a few steps to get the treat after you click.

When you must carry the treats with you, keep them in a fanny pack or bait bag, and get them out one at a time *after* the dog has performed the behavior. Resist the urge to hold several in your hand. If you're going to have to carry the bag of treats often, consider keeping treats on you all the time so your dog won't associate the presence of the treats with work.

Minimize Food Lures

Use a target stick lure instead. Some dogs turn off their brains and focus only on following the food if you use a food lure. If you do use a food lure, fade it quickly, and keep treats off your body.

Once the behavior is on cue, switch from the clicker to a verbal marker and begin using a variety of reinforcers: food, balls, scratches, tug toys, and praise.

Success Story

It took an old dog to show me the most rewarding way to train. I started clicker training with my old Newfoundland, Trixie, when she was eight. She was my crossover girl who hated traditional training. If you even tugged on a leash she would stop, and she didn't seem to be motivated by anything.

Trixie was like a different dog when I started clicker training! I began with simple behaviors. She liked to bring me things, so I trained her to bring me my newspaper. I would click and reward for anything that she brought me. One morning she brought the newspaper, and we went back in the house, where I promptly fell asleep on the couch. I woke up about thirty minutes later and she had covered me with treasures. She brought pot holders, toys, TV remote, slippers and many other items, and just gently laid them on top of me. When I woke up, she was sitting by the couch looking at me like I had won the jackpot!

Susan Kues, New Braunfels, Texas

What's a "crossover" dog?

A crossover dog has previously been trained using another method. These dogs are special, because the method used previously may influence how they react to clicker training.

The most common problem faced by trainers of crossover dogs is a reluctance to offer behavior. Other methods rely heavily on showing the dog what to do; dogs may be lured or physically compelled into performing the behavior. And in some methods, if the dog experiments by offering a behavior that's other than what the trainer wants, she's physically "corrected" for making a mistake.

An over-reliance on either luring or compulsion teaches a dog to be cautious and wait to be shown what to do. The dog never learns to problem solve, to try different options to figure out what will earn a reinforcement. Correcting a dog for mistakes further suppresses the dog's willingness to try alternatives.

Consider, too, that if you have previously trained dogs using another method, you are a crossover trainer. Your journey is at least as difficult as the dog's, and perhaps even more so. Clicker training operates under a completely different set of rules and requires a completely different mindset.

If you've used traditional training methods in the past, it may take time and effort for you to learn not to give automatic corrections for "mistakes." It may also take time for you to begin to look at problems proactively rather than trying to "fix" them. To a traditional trainer, a dog participating as an active member of the learning process can seem out of control. These feelings will pass, however, as you become comfortable with the method and begin to see results.

see also

What do I do when my dog makes a mistake? **page 54**

What do I do if my dog intentionally disobeys a known command? **page 55**

Shouldn't I tell my dog both what he does right and what he does wrong? **page 57**

What does "getting the behavior" mean? **page 76**

Where should I start?

Where to begin depends on many things, including your ultimate goals, your past training experience, your dog's past training experience, your immediate needs or concerns, your dog's age, and the amount of time you've had your dog.

Choose something easy in the beginning. Start with a simple behavior you can capture easily, such as eye contact or a sit. Although you may be excited by the concept of shaping complex behaviors from scratch, train a few basic behaviors first. Shaping is a much more advanced skill.

Clicker trainer Sue Ailsby has two favorite "first" behaviors. Her choice between them depends on the dog:

- Confident, pushy animals need to learn self-control. Sue starts by holding a treat in a closed fist and clicking when the pup stops trying to get the treat. Then she gives him the treat he was trying to get. Lesson: to get what you want, you must give up what you want. The lesson continues with a treat placed on the edge of a table, on a chair, or even on the floor as the dog's level of self-control increases.

- Softer, more cautious dogs need to gain confidence. Sue teaches them to touch (target) her finger. When that behavior is strong, she uses her finger to teach them to target lots of different objects and people. Doing a familiar behavior in an unfamiliar situation helps focus the dog's attention and bolsters confidence.

If your dog already knows basic obedience behaviors, or if you are a cross-over trainer, consider starting with tricks. Trick training is low-pressure, and you won't get quite as frustrated if you make some mistakes along the way.

If you have a new puppy, issues like housebreaking, crate training, and controlling puppy mouthing may top your list. At the same time, you can work on house manners. Sit to be petted. Lots and lots of informal, well-reinforced recalls. Name recognition. Grooming. If you have a new adult dog, these simple acts can help you build a solid relationship with him.

see also

What does "getting the behavior" mean? **page 76**

What is targeting, and why should I do it? **page 118**

How can I get my dog to pay attention to me even in a distracting environment? **page 120**

How do I crate train my dog? **page 140**

How do I stop puppy mouthing? (Bite inhibition training) **page 151**

When you're ready to start with obedience behaviors, begin with attention. Attention is the single most important behavior you can teach your dog, because if you can't get your dog's attention—particularly in distracting situations—you can't get any other behavior either. Attention is the foundation for everything else you teach.

Do my dog's emotions play any part in training?

see also

How do I handle fearful behavior?
page 156

Absolutely!

Your dog's emotions play a big part in how well he will learn. A dog who is extremely frightened, stressed, or angry cannot learn. Even if the dog is only mildly upset, you run the risk of associating that negative emotional state with whatever you're training. You cannot separate emotions from training. You must deal with underlying negative emotions before attempting to modify behavior. Although fear is not the only negative emotion a dog can feel, the method used to address fearful behavior works with any negative emotion.

CHAPTER 6

Punishment, Mistakes, and Errors

Aren't unpleasant consequences a normal part of learning?

Absolutely! Unpleasant consequences can teach an animal to avoid doing certain behaviors or to do something else instead. Touching an electric wire hurts, so the dog learns to avoid the electrified fence. Biting mom when nursing causes mom to stand up and leave, so the pup learns to nurse gently.

Although life is ultimately filled with unpleasant consequences for poor choices, learning new behaviors or even changing old behaviors doesn't have to be painful, scary, or intimidating. The goal of training is a reliable behavior. Whether you use positive reinforcement or corrections, the end result may look the same on the surface, but the difference for the dog will be between enjoying or disliking both the training and the work. Clicker trainers rely on positive reinforcement for good reason.

When I was fifteen, I took a driver's education class in school. I was a typical teen, anxious to drive, thrilled every time my parents let me slip behind the wheel. The instructor of the class yelled at, insulted, embarrassed, and berated students for every mistake. I worked hard to be correct not only because I wanted to do well in the class but because I wanted to escape his torment—a classic example of R-. When the class was over, I put away my keys and didn't drive for over a year. I drive for convenience now, and I am a safe, conscientious driver, but I've never recaptured the joy and excitement I felt before that class.

As far as the driving behaviors themselves are concerned, at this point one might say it didn't matter whether I was taught through R+ or R- because the outcome was that I learned the behaviors and did enough repetitions to make them fluent. But it did matter. Think back through your own learning experiences, both good ones and bad ones. How do you feel about the information you learned during fun learning experiences versus unpleasant ones? Aversives can leave behind a lot of baggage, even when they get the results intended.

see also

What do I do when my dog makes a mistake? **page 54**

What do I do if my dog intentionally disobeys a known command? **page 55**

Shouldn't I tell my dog both what he does right *and* what he does wrong? **page 57**

What is punishment? **page 58**

How do I solve problem behavior? **page 62**

So let me understand this. Even if my dog is running toward a busy street or about to bite someone, I'm not supposed to use punishment? **page 63**

What's the difference between punishment and extinction, which should I use, and why? **page 182**

Sometimes extinction doesn't work. Why not, and what should I do? **page 184**

Don't misunderstand. Just because clicker training doesn't use physical aversives doesn't mean that behaviors don't have consequences. The other questions in this chapter explain more about punishment, including how to handle mistakes during training and how to solve problem behavior. (For more on specific problem behaviors, see Chapter 12; for definitions of behavioral terms, see Chapter 14 and the Glossary.)

> "Don't be so afraid of making a mistake that you never try. The great thing about clicker training is that even if you make a mistake, the worst thing that can happen is that you reward a behavior you don't want. Just don't reward it again, and it will fade away like your mistake never happened.
>
> Angela Pullano, Dayton, OH

What do I do when my dog makes a mistake?

When learning a new behavior, mistakes are inevitable. Part of the learning process is learning that one behavior is right and all other behaviors are wrong. How do we teach this? When the dog does the right behavior, we click and reinforce it. And when the dog does the wrong behavior, we ignore it.

What? Just ignore it?

Yes, clicker trainers ignore mistakes. Why? Because the dog needs to learn that wrong choices are not reinforced. You don't have to punish the behavior. Simply by ignoring the wrong choices your dog makes and judiciously reinforcing the right ones, the right behavior will begin to happen more and more frequently and the dog will make fewer and fewer mistakes.

see also

Aren't unpleasant consequences a normal part of learning? **page 52**

Shouldn't I tell my dog both what he does right and what he does wrong? **page 57**

What's the difference between punishment and extinction, which should I use, and why? **page 182**

Sometimes extinction doesn't work. Why not, and what should I do? **page 184**

What do I do if my dog intentionally
disobeys a known command?

If my dog fails to respond to my cue, I step back and try to figure out why. There are always several possible reasons for a failure to respond:

- *You haven't trained in that location.* Dogs don't generalize like we do. Sit in the kitchen isn't the same as sit in the living room or sit in the yard. The more different places you train the behavior, the better the dog will generalize.

  Steve White, who used to train police dogs for Seattle's police department, trained each behavior from scratch in twenty different locations before he considered it well generalized. Do you have to train in that many locations? Not necessarily, but realize that a dog that hasn't practiced in lots of locations isn't as likely to respond to the cue in a strange location.

- *The dog doesn't know the cue as well as you think.* We are a verbal species and we learn verbal cues easily. Dogs do not. They learn environmental cues, then physical cues, and lastly verbal cues. When adding a verbal cue, it's imperative to make sure nothing nonverbal is also associated with it. Quite often our dogs learn these tiny—even unconscious—physical signals and never learn the verbal cue at all.

  I watched a man in the vet's office. He asked his dog to sit, and his dog remained standing. The man asked again and again, his voice getting louder each time. Finally he screamed and simultaneously touched the dog's back end. The dog dropped into a sit immediately. The dog clearly had a cue for sit, and just as clearly it wasn't what the man thought it was.

  Think about the cue. How often do you give it without getting a response from the dog? Do you routinely say it several times before the dog complies? Do you say it when you don't really care whether the dog does it or not? Every time you use the cue and the dog doesn't do the behavior, you are lessening the effectiveness of the cue.

see also

Aren't unpleasant consequences a normal part of learning? **page 52**

Shouldn't I tell my dog both what he does right and what he does wrong? **page 55**

What is punishment? **page 58**

Are aversives and punishers the same thing? **page 61**

How do I solve problem behavior? **page 62**

So let me understand this. Even if my dog is running toward a busy street or about to bite someone, I'm not supposed to use punishment? **page 63**

Are clicker-trained behaviors reliable? **page 106**

What is "fluent," and how do I get there? **page 112**

At what point does my dog "know" what is being asked of him? **page 116**

- *The dog is distracted by something you haven't trained her to ignore while she's working.* If you want your dog to perform a behavior in the presence of a certain distraction, then you must train in the presence of that kind of distraction. Training in a quiet kitchen will not prepare your dog to do a recall at the dog park. As mentioned above, dogs don't generalize well. However, the more distractions you train against, the more likely the dog is to generalize and ignore a distraction you hadn't anticipated.

- *The dog is stressed.* Even minor stress can affect a dog's reactions. Watch for calming signals: yawning, licking lips, turning face away. Ask for a simple, well-known behavior, and if the dog is capable of that, offer a treat. If he accepts the treat, go through a routine of familiar behaviors to help settle him and give him confidence. If the dog is unable to eat, remove him from the situation. He's too stressed to learn or to perform.

- *You are stressed.* Dogs are incredibly perceptive. If you're stressed or nervous, you don't sound the same or smell the same. Your dog feels your stress and reacts by offering calming signals. Handler stress is frequently a problem in competition obedience. If you need the dog to perform when you're stressed, then you need to find ways to practice when you're stressed.

- *Your dog made a mistake.* Guess what. Mistakes happen. Watch the Olympics and see how few perfect performances you see—and those athletes have willingly devoted their lives to their sport. I've been driving a car with manual transmission for fifteen years, but I still stall it out occasionally. No one is perfect, not even your dog. Cut him some slack.

- *The behavior isn't as reliable as it should be.* This is actually the most common reason a dog fails to respond to a cue. Assess the usual reliability of the behavior in similar circumstances. If you asked ten times, how often would the dog respond? Truly? Most people guess their dog's most reliable behaviors are somewhere between eighty-five and ninety percent reliable. This means that at least one in every ten times, the dog won't respond simply because his training isn't perfect.

All of these reasons for a dog's failure to respond have the same solution: more training. None of them require or deserve punishment or corrections.

Shouldn't I tell my dog both
what he does right *and* what he does wrong?

You are! When you click and treat, you tell your dog he made the right choice. Therefore when you don't click and treat, you're telling him he made a wrong choice and should try something else.

Because humans tend to be terribly reliant on verbal feedback themselves, some trainers add a verbal "*Uh* uh" or "Wrong" as an additional cue. In technical terms, this is called a "no reward marker" or NRM. Although this kind of verbal feedback is well intended, some dogs find it aversive. Thus, instead of providing information, you're actually applying punishment.

Keep your training as simple as possible. Reward all correct choices, and let lack of reinforcement be the only feedback for a mistake. It's easy, and it works!

What do I do when my dog makes a mistake? **page 54**

What do I do if my dog intentionally disobeys a known command? **page 55**

How do I solve problem behavior? **page 62**

What's the difference between punishment and extinction, which should I use, and why? **page 182**

Sometimes extinction doesn't work. Why not, and what should I do? **page 184**

see also

> Since I started clicker training, I yell at my dog a lot less. Using the clicker has made me focus on what works, and I've observed that my years of yelling had (at best) no lasting effect on the behavior I was trying to change. Was I even trying to change it? Perhaps I was just trying to let my dog know I didn't like that behavior. Now I concentrate on the best way to communicate what behavior I do like.
>
> Erica Nance, New York City, NY

What is punishment?

The term *punishment* carries certain connotations in American society. If someone wrongs another, we call for—demand—a form of punishment that involves something bad happening to the offender. Criminals are punished, as are rebellious children.

Though we often claim to be punishing bad behavior in order to stop it from happening again, inflicting one kind of pain or another may not actually reduce the frequency of the behavior. Ask any class troublemaker how often he's been sent to the office to be "punished." Prison is one of our most severe punishments, but the vast majority of criminals become repeat offenders.

In clicker training, punishment has nothing to do with retribution, vengeance, or retaliation because your dog has "been bad." Clicker trainers rarely use the word "punishment" at all, but when they do they have in mind a more complex definition based on the vocabulary of behavioral science. In operant conditioning, punishment means only "adding or taking away something that reduces the frequency of a behavior over time."

By this definition, a behavior can be punished by *adding* an aversive, something an individual will work to avoid, or by removing something that he or she wants. These alternatives are more precisely referred to as positive punishment (P+) and negative punishment (P-). In everyday language, positive and negative commonly mean good and bad. However, in clicker training, think of the plus and the minus as mathematical signs, adding or subtracting something in order to change behavior.

We are most familiar with the concept of adding an aversive as a punisher. Spanking, yelling, and speeding tickets are examples of adding something a person doesn't like in order to stop unwanted behavior. In traditional dog training, the handler is advised to jerk the dog's collar, spray water in its face, make a loud noise with a shaker can of pennies or pebbles, or even apply electric shock. All of these are examples of positive punishment.

The other type of punishment is negative punishment. This involves taking away something desirable. Naughty schoolchildren miss recess. Teenagers might be grounded for missing curfew. On a more serious level (and to protect others), people who drive while drunk lose their licenses.

This is the only type of punishment used in clicker training. Why? Negative punishment doesn't rely on fear, pain, or intimidation. Even more importantly, negative punishment can be tied to a positive reinforcer, making the connection between *behavior* and *consequences* incredibly clear.

For example, Bentley, a darling soft-coated wheaten terrier in one of my classes, jumped on people to elicit petting and attention. His owner and I worked out a plan. The owner instructed people to turn and walk away, removing the attention the dog craved at the moment he jumped. When Bentley sat, the people were told to come forward and pet him, giving him the reinforcer *he* wanted for the behavior *his owner* wanted. If the dog sat, he got what he wanted. If he jumped, he lost what he wanted.

But obviously, positive punishment—the use of aversives—may also work. Why, then, don't clicker trainers use it more frequently?

First of all, aversives suppress behavior. In order to train, you need to get behavior. Dogs who are punished for mistakes become reluctant to offer anything new.

Second, even used correctly, aversives may have side-effects, including fear and aggression.

Third, aversives are difficult to apply correctly. In order to be effective, this form of punishment must meet *all* of the following criteria:

- *The punishment must occur the moment the undesired behavior occurs.* If you delay more than two seconds, it's likely to be associated with something other than that behavior. For example, a dog tears something up, and when her owner gets home he gets angry. Instead of associating the

Food for Thought

When learning clicker training, the most difficult thing has been trying to change my own behaviors. When I started clicker training with Diesel I was constantly bashing myself if I did something wrong. I was angry at myself. I told myself what an idiot I was and huffily told myself never to do that again. I really gave myself a hard time.

Well, that has changed. These days, when I do something wrong it often makes me feel bad, but instead of scolding myself, I start thinking about what caused the situation. Could I have done something differently? Could I have avoided the situation altogether? If not, why did I do what I do? Would it be possible to behave differently? And what surprises me is I do it calmly, assuring myself I will do better the next time.

Laura I. Kansanen, Helsinki, Finland

anger and subsequent punishment with the chewing, the dog associates it with the homecoming and thus begins to "look guilty" when her owner comes in because she anticipates an angry outburst.

- *The punishment must be associated with the behavior, not the trainer, training, or something else in the environment.* For instance, prong collars, though they give perfectly timed corrections, also give the correction whenever the dog lunges toward something, such as another dog that's approaching. Your dog may associate the correction with the other dog instead of with his lunge, thus leading to on-leash aggression.

- *The punishment must be stronger than the reinforcer associated with doing the undesired behavior.* A lot of male dogs will gladly suffer the shock of an electric fence to get to a bitch in heat on the other side.

- *The punishment must be severe enough to stop the behavior almost immediately.* If you are going to use an aversive as punishment, you should have to apply it no more than three times. If the behavior persists beyond that, you're doing something wrong. One of the worst things you can do is apply constant low-level punishers. This nagging desensitizes the dog to physical corrections, meaning you'll have to use stronger and stronger punishers for even mild problems.

- *The animal must have the opportunity to change its behavior.* You must give your dog a way out by watching closely for alternative behaviors that are acceptable and reinforcing them immediately. Otherwise punishment is purely a manner of suppressing behavior—it is in no way instructive.

- *The behavior must be controllable.* Punishing a young puppy for wetting in the house does nothing but frighten and confuse the puppy. It's not yet capable of controlling its bladder. It will wet wherever it is when it needs to go.

One important thing to remember about punishment by any definition is that all punishment is aversive, even negative punishment. While aversives may be mild or are severe, they are only effective when the dog finds them unpleasant and is willing to work to avoid them. Fortunately, the vast majority of training can be accomplished without using any punishment. In my experience, except in an emergency, what works best to lessen undesirable behavior is to ignore it while simultaneously strengthening an alternative, desired behavior.

Are aversives and punishers the same thing?

All punishers are aversives, but all aversives are not necessarily punishers.

An aversive is something the dog will work to avoid. A punisher is an aversive that suppresses or lessens the likelihood of the occurrence of a specific behavior over time.

Ansel is an energetic Siberian husky who used to drag his owner down the street on walks. His owner took him to an obedience class and learned to "correct" him—to jerk on his choke-style collar—whenever he forged ahead. Ansel would forge, the owner would pop the collar, Ansel would fall back for a step or two, then forge ahead again.

The collar pops were undeniably aversive. In fact, when his owner complained to the instructor that the pops didn't seem to work, the instructor demonstrated how to give a correction hard enough to make the dog yelp. But still the forging behavior continued.

The collar pops were aversive, but they were not, by definition, a punisher for Ansel. Like reinforcers, punishers are defined by the results they achieve, and what is a punisher for one dog (or in one situation) may not be a punisher for (or in) another. Some dogs might have quit forging to avoid the pops, but not Ansel.

Unfortunately, the collar pops, though ineffective as a punisher, were not harmless. Each pop added stress to the situation. Over time, the stress built and built until finally Ansel couldn't take it anymore. He retaliated by trying to bite his owner. The owner countered with more severe corrections, but that only made the problem worse.

Fortunately, Ansel's owner recognized that the method he was using wasn't working and sought help from a different trainer. The trainer he contacted helped repair the damaged relationship and recommended clicker training. Today Ansel is a happy, unaggressive Siberian who walks nicely on a loose leash.

see also

What is punishment? **page 58**

How do I solve
problem behavior?

see also

Aren't unpleasant consequences a normal part of learning? **page 52**

What does "getting the behavior" mean? **page 76**

What is management? How do I "set my dog up for success"? **page 166**

Solving problem behavior—any problem behavior—is a four-step process:

1. *Identify the behavior you don't like.* Be specific. Describing your dog as "too hyper" or as a brat doesn't really say what you want to change. Instead, try statements like "I don't like my dog to jump on people" or "I don't like my dog to pull on the leash."

2. *Determine what you want the dog to do instead.* It's not enough to say you want the problem behavior to stop. Your dog could stop that behavior and choose to do something even worse! Save yourself time— and your dog confusion—by defining what it is that you do want your dog to do in this situation. For example, if your dog jumps on people, you might decide you want her to sit to be petted instead. If your dog pulls on the leash, you'd probably prefer that she learn to walk at your side, ignoring distractions.

3. *Manage the situation so the unwanted behavior becomes unreinforcing or impossible.* This step is critical to the process. Every time your dog successfully does the unwanted behavior, he's reinforcing it—making it more likely to occur again in the future. Your job as trainer is to figure out what triggers the behavior and anticipate it, to be proactive and prepared. Let's say you know your dog jumps on people who come through the front door. So when someone comes to the door, plan ahead and put your dog on a leash. You might also ask the visitor to stand perfectly still unless the dog is seated. If you don't have time to work on the behavior, set your dog up to succeed by putting him in another room, thereby making it impossible for him to jump on the visitor.

4. *Train the new, preferred behavior.* Train the substitute behavior like any other, making sure to reinforce every correct repetition. Also remember that when dealing with problem behavior, the best reinforcer is always the one that worked as the payoff the dog was getting for the unwanted behavior in the past. The dog who jumped was getting attention and

petting. When a visitor comes, he doesn't want a food treat. He wants attention! So make sure he gets that, but only in exchange for doing what you want.

Note that I never mentioned physically correcting the problem behavior. It simply isn't necessary to collar pop, alpha roll, yell, spray the dog in the face, knee it in the chest, or grab its muzzle. Be proactive, not reactive. Don't set up an adversarial relationship. Find a solution that is mutually rewarding.

So let me understand this.
Even if my dog is running toward a busy street or about to bite someone, I'm not supposed to use punishment?

These are not training exercises. These are unexpected emergency situations that require immediate, dire action. You must do whatever is necessary to protect your dog, yourself, and the people and animals around you.

However, once the emergency is passed, take the time to figure out why it happened in the first place. Why was a dog without a totally reliable recall loose near a busy road? Why did your dog feel stressed enough to bite—and why didn't you recognize the signs of stress ahead of time? Most importantly, what can you do to prevent that situation from ever occurring again?

Finally, understand that all actions have consequences. Even emergency actions. Tackling the runaway dog may save his life, but if that dog is skittish to begin with, that one action might set your relationship and his training back days, weeks, or months. Be alert for such damage and ready to work to repair it.

What is management? How do I "set my dog up for success"? **page 166**

see also

I've read that I should mimic wolves
to communicate that I'm displeased with my dogs. Is this true?

see also

How do I build a good relationship with my dog? **page 164**

What is management? How do I "set my dog up for success"? **page 166**

How can I know when my dog is stressed, and what can I do about it? **page 170**

How can I establish myself as the "leader" in my home? **page 174**

Humans don't make very good wolves—or very good dogs, for that matter.

Dogs have an incredibly rich language, a great deal of which is subtle, silent body language. In addition to the overt barks and growls and obvious posturing we're used to seeing and hearing about, dogs communicate through behaviors like a minor change in breathing pattern or an arced, rather than direct, approach to another dog.

These subtle signals are the language of peace. When one dog reprimands another, the second dog communicates understanding with just lick of the lips or a glance away. Instantly, the aggression ends. Communication achieved.

Humans tend to want to mimic the overt aggressive language of dogs without learning the subtle, peaceful one. This is the equivalent of attempting to communicate in a foreign language using only the swear words. We growl, scruff shake, and alpha roll without recognizing the signs of surrender. We leave our animal terrified—or with no choice but to fight back.

Forget about using dog language to communicate your displeasure. If you want to learn more about how dogs communicate, learn the language of peace, a vocabulary of gestures called calming signals by Turid Rugaas, a researcher who documented them. (See "Resources" at the end of this book.) As you become fluent, you'll find you don't really need the swear words anyway.

CHAPTER 7 About Training Sessions

How long should I train at one time?

When you train, you want to get maximum results for the least effort. Therefore, keep training periods short to take advantage of a fresh, ready-to-learn brain. When deciding how long to train at one time, consider the following:

- *Your dog's age.* Puppies have a short attention span. Frequent, short periods work best with young puppies. Training for thirty seconds, a minute, or two minutes is plenty. Then take a break and play a game. As your dog gets older, she'll develop a longer attention span.

- *Your dog's experience.* Dogs must learn to concentrate. A dog that's new to clicker training is going to have to work a lot harder mentally to understand what's happening. So train for short periods of perhaps two or three minutes at first. Once the dog understands clicker training, she'll be able to focus all of her concentration on learning the behavior you're teaching and won't find training as tiring mentally.

- *The newness of the behavior you're training.* Figuring out a new behavior requires more mental effort than perfecting a better known one. So until a behavior is strongly on cue, keep training periods short—two or three minutes.

An experienced older dog perfecting a well-known behavior is capable of working for longer. However, unless you have a pressing need for longer periods, keep them between five and ten minutes. According to Bob Bailey, after ten minutes the learning curve begins to taper off and you'll get less bang for your buck.

> Probably the hardest thing for me in clicker training is remembering that *this is stressful to the dog.* Not in a bad way, of course—my dogs absolutely love to see the clicker come out, and they love to earn clicks. But this is a hard-thinking activity. It's my job to make sure they don't burn out or get frustrated, and if they need to back off for a few minutes or a few hours to "process," that's fine, too.
>
> Laura VanArendonk Baugh, Indianapolis, IN

How often should I train?

Your dog needs a break between training periods, but that break can be as short as a few minutes. For most people, the problem isn't training too frequently but how they can possibly fit the whole project of dog training into their busy schedules.

Can I train more than one behavior at a time? How many behaviors can I train during a training period? **page 68**

see also

Here are some ideas for making time to train:

- Train during the commercial breaks of your favorite TV shows. One commercial break equals one training period.
- Train for two or three minutes before feeding the dog
- If you take your dog out on leash to potty, train for two or three minutes after your dog relieves himself
- Stop every hundred yards on your regular walk and hold a thirty-second or one-minute training session

You can also accomplish a great deal by working common obedience behaviors into your daily routine:

- sit-stays at doorways instead of bolting through
- sit-stays when the doorbell rings and guests arrive
- ignoring dropped food or forbidden "delicacies" found outside
- sitting to be petted when people approach on walks
- down-stay or "settle" on mat while the family eats dinner or while guests are present
- sit-stay while you prepare the dog's food
- easy handling by you, the vet, or a professional groomer
- no-hassle walks on the leash, no matter what the distraction
- polite behavior when passing or being passed by other dogs
- reliable recalls in unexpected, possibly dangerous situations
- waiting until cued to exit the car

Can I train more than one behavior at a time?
How many behaviors can I train during one training period?

see also

How long should I train at one time?
page 66

How often should I train? **page 67**

You can work on as many different behaviors as you want. Evaluate what's most important to you. You get out of a behavior what you put into it. A behavior that is trained several times a day is going to progress faster than one that's practiced just once a day. If you need a reliable sit, then spend more time working on that than on "balance a cookie on your nose."

If you're working on multiple behaviors, try to arrange it so that the different behaviors are in different stages of training. Initial learning is more stressful than the proofing stage, when behaviors are trained for reliability even amidst distractions, because learning is more concentration-intensive.

To minimize confusion, keep your training periods short, and stick to one behavior per training period until several behaviors are strongly on cue. If you really need to work on more than one behavior during a single period, make it obvious to the dog you're going to do something different. Physical cues are very important to dogs, so take a short play break between sessions and start working on the next behavior in a different room or location.

When I start a training session,
my dog "throws" all of the behaviors he knows at me.
Am I damaging these behaviors if I don't reinforce them?

If a behavior is not reinforced it will eventually disappear. (This is known as extinction.) However, as long as you continue to reinforce the behavior in other training sessions, you won't damage it by ignoring it when you don't want it.

When you start a training session, it's up to you to define exactly what will and won't earn a click during that session. If you are working on a down, ignore all other behaviors, or reinforce them only minimally. After you have been working heavily on one particular behavior, it may take an effort to get a new and different one. You may have to lure or lower your criteria—your definition of what earns a click—to the most basic beginnings of the response you're after. Stick with it. Your dog will eventually catch on that new behaviors can also earn rewards, and that it's the click that tells her what to do.

What do you mean by "criteria"?
page 78

When should I click? (How do I choose my criteria?) **page 79**

see also

> Watch other clicker trainers. Watch when they click. Try to figure out what their criteria is while they're clicking. Look at how small they break the behaviors down. Pay attention to the path they take through shaping to get the behavior they wanted. Ask them why they chose that path!
>
> Michele Stone, La Jolla, CA

Should I keep records?

see also

What do you mean by "criteria"?
page 78

When should I click? (How do I choose my criteria?) **page 79**

How do I know when to "make it harder"—increase my criteria for training? **page 80**

Keeping a record of your training will help you know exactly what you've trained and exactly how your dog is performing. Keeping records can only help you. If something isn't working, a record lets you go back and figure out why. It helps you see, objectively, what's happening.

Suggested fields for training records include:

• behavior being trained

• date

• session start and end times

• specific criteria for the session

• number of responses/number of errors

• notes

Although recording your data between sessions does take time, using that information to evaluate your last session and plan your next one enables you to make your training more efficient. In particular it helps prevent you from spending either too much or too little time on any one criterion as you work with your dog to perfect a behavior.

My dog gets bored easily. What should I do?

A dog that loses interest in the middle of a training session is often labeled "bored." But a loss of interest may stem from several problems, all of which can be easily solved:

- *Low rate of reinforcement.* How much time is elapsing between successful repetitions? Set your criteria low enough that your dog is successful often enough to remain interested in the game.

- *The use of a low-quality reinforcer.* Does the dog want what you're offering? A reinforcer is something your dog is willing to work for in a given situation. Your dog may find something else in the environment more interesting. You may need to train in a different place or use something more desirable as reinforcement.

- *Predictability.* It's easy for the dog to weigh his options if he knows exactly what he's going to get for playing the game. Consider mixing a variety of low, medium, and high value reinforcers, so he won't ever be quite sure what he's getting next.

- *Stress.* A lack of interest in training may actually be a sign of a stressed dog. Sources of stress include the following:

  * Brain overload. Learning is inherently stressful. Keep training periods short and give your dog a chance to process what he has learned.
  * Your attitude. It's easy for us to get very serious during training sessions, even when things are going well. After all, we're concentrating! And your body language may be quite different if *you* feel stressed, communicating this mood to your dog. Try to stay relaxed and make training fun for both of you.
  * The environment. Look for potential triggers around you. Try moving to a different location and trying again.

- *Confusion.* If your dog is confused by your own poor timing, unclear criteria, or other such trainer errors, he may simply give up.

see also

What if I can't offer a food treat or if my dog isn't interested in the reward I'm offering? **page 33**

Is the timing of the click important? How can I improve my timing? **page 44**

What do I do when my dog makes a mistake? **page 54**

What do you mean by "criteria"? **page 78**

When should I click? (How do I choose my criteria?) **page 79**

How do I know when to "make it harder"—increase my criteria for training? **page 80**

I set my criteria, but my dog advanced a lot further than that. Should I raise my criteria accordingly? **page 83**

I have more than one dog.
Can I train them at the same time?

Yes… and no.

One of the keys to success is controlling your training environment. Train new behaviors in quiet locations with no distractions. Add distractions and new locations systematically and gradually.

Having another dog present during training is incredibly distracting! Working in the presence of other dogs is definitely possible, but any distraction needs to be added slowly and deliberately. To have another dog loose and competing for attention during a training session practically guarantees neither you nor your dogs will get the most out of that session.

Set you and your dogs up to succeed. Work with one dog at a time. Either crate the others or put them in a separate room out of sight. Once you are a more advanced trainer and the dogs are experienced clicker dogs, you can have more than one dog working at the same time by having one hold a stay while you work with the other. However, even then you will probably find that when introducing a new behavior you're a better trainer and your dog is a better learner if you minimize distractions.

Don't be surprised if you observe your dogs employing trained behaviors while interacting with each other!

Success Story

Last month I was having fun shaping a crawl with Maxwell. A couple days after the shaping session, my husband and I were watching TV with Maxwell on the floor and Sassy, the eight-year-old mix on the chair. We noticed a very peculiar movement on the floor. Maxwell was crawling! What in the world was that for? We watched in fascination as he crawled in a semi circle to Sassy's prized rawhide! What a rascal. He used his trick to get Sassy's most prized possession without a scene. She just blinked. He got to chew it. I thought I was just having fun teaching the dogs little tricks. Little did I know the dogs were thinking up ways to use them!

Katherine Yata, Newbury Park, CA

How do I end a training session?

You don't have to have a formal ending. Just finish your session, give your dog a pat, and tell him, "That's all." If you want, play a game with him or just relax together.

Some trainers like to end with a jackpot—a whole handful of treats or an especially desirable reinforcer. As long as you're not inadvertently reinforcing a substandard performance, a jackpot won't hurt anything. So if it makes you feel good, go for it! It isn't necessary, though.

If you're timing your training periods, set any timer you use to go off a minute or so early. That way the sound of the timer won't become a signal for the immediate end of the session.

How long should I train at one time? **page 66**

How often should I train? **page 67**

What's a jackpot, and when should I give one? **page 189**

see also

> My dog was scared of the laundry basket. So I clicked and treated her for interacting with it to get her over her fear. Well, without thinking, I taught her to knock it over. So before long she was knocking it over when it was full—not too smart after folding the clothes...
>
> Amy Dunphy, Manassas, VA

CHAPTER 8 Getting the Behavior

What does "getting the behavior" mean?

see also

What do you mean by "criteria"?
page 78

When should I click? (How do I choose my criteria?) **page 79**

How do I begin shaping?**page 84**

My dog doesn't "offer" behaviors. How can I clicker train?**page 86**

How do I shape a complex behavior, such as a fast, straight, square sit? **page 88**

How do I train a chain of behaviors, such as a formal retrieve? **page 90**

In order to clicker train, you must first have something to reinforce, therefore the first rule of training is to "get the behavior." Obviously, your dog won't perform a precise, refined behavior out of the blue. You'll need to start with something rougher—perhaps even a just small portion of the behavior you want to train—and then gradually shape it and put it on cue.

There are four ways to get the initial behavior:

- *Modeling* is a technique used in traditional training. At the outset, the dog is physically guided—or otherwise compelled—into doing the behavior. Pushing a dog's rear into a sit is modeling. Clicker trainers don't use modeling because we want our dogs to be active participants in the training process, using their own brains to figure out what will earn them clicks.

- *Luring* is a hands-off method of guiding the dog through a behavior. For example, a food lure can be used to guide a dog from a sit into a down. This is a common method of getting more complex behaviors. Lures are usually food, but they may also be target sticks or anything else the dog will follow. Trainers must take care to fade the lure early.

- *Capturing* is an excellent method for training simple, naturally occurring behaviors. The trainer waits for the dog to offer the behavior, then marks and rewards it. A trainer wanting to train a dog to lie down would wait for the dog to lie down to rest, then click and treat.

- *Shaping* is a technique for training a more complex behavior by identifying, rewarding, and gradually building upon its individual components. For example, to shape a spin, you would start by clicking and reinforcing a glance to the right, then a head turn in the same direction, then turn plus the movement of one paw, and so on until the dog is turning all the way around. Shaping also enables clicker trainers to train for precision—a consistently neat sit, for example, rather than a sloppy one.

Some people believe that the only "legitimate" way to clicker train is by using capturing and shaping exclusively. Hogwash. Remember step number one: "Get the behavior." If every behavior had to be shaped from scratch, training would take forever. When training complex behaviors that show little relation to commonly offered behavior, it's often much more efficient to lure the initial behavior and use shaping to refine it.

Does that mean it's a waste of time to shape behavior from scratch? Of course not. Free shaping is a great way to hone your timing and criteria-setting skills, and it's an excellent way to teach your dog to look to the clicker as a source of information. Shaping teaches your dog to think in a way that luring does not and makes him an active, equal partner in the training process.

Success Story

My bluetick hound, Jenny, was offering wild leaps. Because it was winter and I was looking for a good way to burn energy, I was clicking some of the more energetic ones. Jenny was having a blast and I was laughing so hard that tears were coming to my eyes. I clicked one particularly exuberant leap just as Jenny went BONK head first into one of the support beams in the living room.

Now Jenny is very quick to pick up what she got clicked for. Precision is important to her. She will go through every behavior she thinks she has ever gotten clicked for in rapid succession as soon as she sees the clicker come out. Much to my chagrin, the next session we started, the first thing she did was go BONK right into the pole! I called her to me, afraid she had hurt herself, and she gave me that "What did I do wrong, mom—let's go" look and went BONK again!

I knew that it had to hurt, but she didn't care; she wanted that click. It was months before she stopped offering that BONK. I learned my lesson that day and am much more careful when I click her. She still gets clicks for her wild leaps when I want her to burn off some energy but now they aren't [given] until after she has all four on the floor and turns to face me. [And] if she runs into something, no click!

Lisa Yanchunis, Black Hawk, CO

"The tip I remember most was that talking to my dog during training would be like someone chattering to me while I was trying to do long division in my head. Not necessarily impossible, but a LOT harder.

Deb Boyken, Denville, NJ

What do you mean by "criteria"?

see also

How do I know when to "make it harder"—increase my criteria for training? **page 90**

I set my criteria, but my dog advanced a lot further than that. Should I raise my criteria accordingly? **page 82**

A final, finished behavior is often very complex. Not only may be the behavior itself be quite complicated, but there are additional elements such as duration, distance, generalization to different locations, and proofing against a variety of distractions. Both the initial behavior and each of these elements must be attended to bit by bit.

When you're training, you should know exactly what bit you're looking for in each session. This "bit" is a criterion (plural: criteria). Your criterion is defined by you at the beginning of each session. It must be specific and consistent throughout the session, which means that:

• during that set of repetitions you will click only behavior that meets that criterion

• you will click at the moment the dog meets your criterion

At the end of the session, you can review your data and determine whether you're ready to move ahead.

Some examples of session criteria include:

• eye contact of one second with other dogs present

• tucked sits

• touching a target with a paw

• holding a stay when a dog walks past three feet away

• targeting a scented object in a pile of unscented objects

When should I click?

(How do I choose my criteria?)

When you click depends on what you're trying to reinforce at a particular moment. To make matters more confusing, when to click will change many, many times as you shape a behavior.

When you first begin working on sit, you click the sit itself—the moment the dog's rear end touches the floor. Soon she's sitting regularly, but she gets up as soon as you click. So you want to add duration to the behavior. Now you click a second after the sit. Then you wait for two seconds, then four. After a few days, she's holding her sit quite reliably, except when people walk by. So you change the timing of the click again, clicking only at the moment an approaching person passes by.

In all of these examples, when to click is determined by your criterion for a particular training session. When to click is actually quite simple: you click at the instant your dog achieves your criterion.

Setting criteria is one of the most basic—and most difficult—skills a clicker trainer must learn. Improperly defined criteria are frequently at the root of training problems. Defining your criterion is easiest when the behavior is black and white. For example, touching a target. Either the dog touches it or she doesn't, and it's easy to figure out exactly when to click—when the dog's paw (or nose) touches the stick.

Unfortunately, not all criteria are that clear. For example, you're training your dog to hit a bell to let you know when she wants to go outside. She's targeting the bell, but she needs to hit it harder. "Harder" is not black and white. A clearer criterion might be "hard enough to make the bell move one inch to the side" or "hard enough to make it ring twice."

In the beginning, make your job as easy as possible—stick to clear, discrete criteria as much as possible.

see also

How do I know when to "make it harder"—increase my criteria for training? **page 80**

How do I begin shaping? **page 84**

My dog doesn't "offer" behaviors. How can I clicker train? **page 86**

How do I shape a complex behavior, such as a fast, straight, square sit? **page 88**

How do I train a chain of behaviors, such as a formal retrieve? **page 90**

How do I know when to "make it harder"—
increase my criteria for training?

see also

What do I do when my dog makes a mistake? **page 54**

I set my criteria, but my dog advanced a lot further than that. Should I raise my criteria accordingly? **page 82**

If you stay at one criterion too long, it can be difficult to move past it because your dog has such a strong reinforcement history for that response. However, if you increase your criteria too quickly your dog may become confused, and the behavior may fall apart. Fortunately, if you keep simple records it's easy to tell when to increase your criteria. The data will tell you!

Step #1: Set your criterion. Remember, it must be specific.

Step #2: Do ten repetitions of the behavior. This is one training session. Click if, and only if, your dog achieves your criterion. If he doesn't, count that repetition as an error.

Step #3: At the end of the session, count the number of errors.

Temporary criteria are criteria that won't be present in the finished behavior. For example, say your ultimate goal is a recall from at least a hundred feet away, but currently your dog is working on recalls from fifteen feet. Fifteen feet is a temporary criterion you're using to shape recalls of up to a hundred feet.

Permanent criteria are elements that are present in the finished behavior. For example, a competition-quality sit must be tucked, which means the front feet remain still and the rear feet are brought in and under. "Tucked" is part of the finished behavior, so you want to make this criterion more reliable before adding something else.

Keep your eye on your data and adjust it accordingly:

• If your criterion was a temporary one and your dog made two or fewer errors in ten reps (80 percent or more correct responses in the session), you can increase your criteria.

- If your criterion was a permanent one, aim for a higher percentage of correct responses (ninety percent or better) before moving on—one or fewer errors in ten reps.

- If your dog made more errors, stay at the same criteria for the next session.

- If your dog makes more than two incorrect responses in a row, *stop* and reevaluate your criteria. Don't frustrate your dog or yourself.

Once you've increased your criteria, don't back up. Your dog would *love* not to work so hard for a click. At the beginning of a training period, she may indeed try offering a lesser version of the behavior. If you accept that behavior, she will quickly train you to make it easier for her. Stick to your guns and trust your data.

Using the percentage of correct responses like this enables you to make your training extremely efficient. You won't increase too quickly, building a weak behavior and confusing your dog, nor too slowly, making it hard to move past a heavily reinforced temporary criteria.

Note: "Backing up" means repeating holding your dog to a lesser standard in the same situation; it is not the same thing as relaxing your requirements temporarily in a new one. When you add a new distraction, a new location, or another new element, you can relax your standards for the previous elements a bit until the dog gets comfortable what's new, then gradually tighten them up again to bring all of the elements together into a smooth, precise performance.

Food for Thought

Observe. Just sit down and watch. Make notes if you want to, but just watch what the animal does and how it does it. Don't assume what the animal is feeling, just watch what it does, what kind of behaviors lead to what [other] behaviors. All the very basics of clicker training—timing, criteria, rate of reinforcement—require observation skills.

At first, it was so difficult to see how the most basic behaviors could be split into small fractions. Observation helped me to see what my dog really does, how she does it, what kind of things might precede certain behaviors. I needed to learn to see what one small behavior consists of—turning head, lifting a leg, shifting butt, that one small thing that might be a start to the complete behavior. Another difficult thing was timing. How to catch that tiny reaction! Again, observing how my dog moves helped tremendously. Of course, timing doesn't improve without practice, but observing, getting yourself used to the way the animals move and behave, can help you get started.

Laura I. Kansanen, Helsinki, Finland

I set my criteria, but my dog advanced a lot further than that.
Should I raise my criteria accordingly?

This is a very common occurrence. You're carefully progressing step by step, then suddenly the dog jumps ahead and performs well beyond your expectations. For example, you've been shaping a spin. You started with a glance to the right. Then a head turn. Then a step with the front foot. Suddenly the dog turns a third of the way around. Then he does it again! You're sure he has this figured out.

What do you do? Do you take advantage of this "leap of learning" and advance to the new level of competency?

No. Very often the offering doesn't reveal true understanding of what you want. Trainers who jump ahead like this often find the behavior falls apart later.

Stick to your current criterion throughout this session. If indeed the dog is consistently performing beyond what's expected, your percentage of correct responses will be high enough to justify moving ahead the next time you train. At that point, increase your criteria in the same small increment you would use even if the dog hadn't performed beyond your expectations. Again, if the dog has truly made a leap of learning, he'll fly through this set of repetitions with a high percentage of correct responses and you'll be ready to move on. If not, you haven't risked confusing your dog by going too fast.

see also

How do I know when to "make it harder"—increase my criteria for training? **page 86**

Food for Thought

I was teaching Cassie to drop a toy into a box. I shaped the behavior with the box in front of me. She started lowering her head into the box after dropping the toy over it, and I started clicking that because it seemed like a stronger orientation to getting the toy into the box. Then I moved the box a few inches to the side of me. Cassie walked up to me, dropped the toy on the floor in front of me, then stepped to the box and stuck her head inside it.

Wendy S. Katz, Lexington, KY

I set my criteria, but now I'm getting few correct responses.
Will he get better with more practice?

It only makes sense that when you raise criteria the number of correct responses will drop. However, the dog should still be successful the majority of the time. If the dog makes more than two mistakes in a row or has a 50 percent (or lower) error rate for the session, stop training for that behavior until you reevaluate what you're doing.

The dog should not just be successful; he should be successful quickly and often. For optimal learning you need a high rate of reinforcement. If your rate of reinforcement drops too low, either because the dog isn't successful or because you fail to reinforce correct behaviors, your dog may become frustrated or quit.

Set your criteria at an achievable level and don't increase them until your dog's behavior is reliable at the current level.

What do you mean by "criteria"? **page 78**

When should I click? (How do I choose my criteria?) **page 879**

How do I know when to "make it harder"—increase my criteria for training? **page 80**

see also

> Write down everything that your dog does in five minutes. A head turn to the left, a head dip, a scratch, a nose lick, and so on. It really makes you notice all the little things.
>
> Stephanie Weaver, Midway Park, NC

How do I begin shaping?

Have you ever attended a dolphin show? Have you ever sat spellbound watching the animals jump and spin and dance on their tails? Did you wonder how the trainer trained these behaviors? Tail-dancing is most certainly not a naturally occurring behavior that can be captured in its entirety; nor can a dolphin trainer put a collar on the animal and lift it out of the water. Even holding out a fish as a lure doesn't get you very far.

Instead, the trainer likely started with whatever tiny beginning she saw—perhaps just a nose out of the water—and gradually, through judicious, planned reinforcement, built that into the entire performance: body out of the water, balanced on the tail, dancing backwards. The dolphin trainer shaped the behavior "from scratch," as clicker trainers say.

Why, if dog trainers can model and lure, would we ever want to go to the trouble of shaping a behavior from scratch? As noted earlier in this chapter, it's often more time efficient to lure the initial behavior and use shaping just to refine and perfect it.

But free-shaping behavior—that is, beginning with something the animal does on its own—gives you something that luring cannot: it gives you a thinking dog who is as actively involved in the training game as you are. A free-shaped dog knows his behavior causes the click, and he actively experiments to earn that click.

If your dog has previously been taught using modeling or luring—or if you are accustomed to using those methods—free-shaping can be a challenge. Your dog has learned to wait to be shown what to do. You've learned to "help" him figure things out. Here are some suggestions and exercises to help you "get behavior" by encouraging your dog to think on its own:

1. Stop luring. Completely. Totally.

2. Start by clicking for the simplest behavior you can think of. For example, click the movement of one front foot. Once the dog is moving that foot more frequently, shape the paw lift higher and higher.

3. Next, shape your dog to something—anything—with a chair. Put out a chair and click your dog's interactions with it. Then pick one behavior and shape it.

4. Pick a random spot in the room and shape your dog to go to that spot. Or pick an object and shape your dog to target (touch) it.

I demonstrated basic shaping to a friend of mine, and she said, "Wouldn't it be easier just to…" Yes, it would. The object of these early games isn't the specific behavior but the experience of learning in this way. I don't care if my dog raises his paw, walks around a chair, or targets the planter in the corner. What is important is that my dog actively works to figure out what I want, that he actively tries to solve the problem.

Problem solving may not be necessary for a dog who rarely leaves the house and meets few people other than his immediate family. But any dog who is taken into unfamiliar circumstances—particularly a competition or working dog—will benefit from learning to work through unexpected events instead of waiting for guidance.

Success Story

I clicker trained my standard poodle (who is now an Australian Obedience Champion) from puppyhood. When she was three and a half years old, I decided to teach her agility. I decided I would clicker train the weave poles. She was clicked for making the correct entries, clicked for going from end to end, clicked for quickness, etc. Everything was going smoothly until the weaving poles were finally placed totally upright in a competition line. Suddenly she couldn't weave. If I slightly sloped the poles, away she would go. I was stumped…

Then I thought to myself, "She's clicker trained. Let her think it out herself!" So I stood three meters away, clicker in hand, arms folded, and waited. Minutes went by and she ran to the poles, ran down the outside line of the poles, ran down the other side of the poles, did entries, weaved a couple of poles, sat at the poles, lay down, touched the poles with her nose, tried a few more entries. Then she backed away from the poles and with a sudden burst of speed threw herself into a perfect entry and weaved the twelve poles flat out! CLICK! JACKPOT!

Gina O'Keefe, Perth, Western Australia

My dog doesn't "offer" behaviors.
How can I clicker train?

Some dogs, particularly crossover dogs, don't show much creativity when it comes to offering behavior. Many just sit and wait to be shown what to do. This reluctance to offer behavior can frustrate clicker trainers—there's seemingly no new behavior to work with. If your dog is a reluctant offerer, the following tips might help reawaken his or her creativity:

• *Carry your clicker with you outside of formal sessions, and click (and reinforce) any behavior your dog offers frequently.* For example, perhaps your dog offers a natural stack—an alert but composed standing position much desired in the conformation ring. Click and treat whenever you see your dog do that behavior until it's offered in order to solicit the click and treat. In other words, turn a spontaneous offering into a formal training session for that behavior.

• *Be flexible.* If you're working with a crossover dog, back off and be less rigid in your training plan until the dog learns the new method. When you start a training period, click and treat whatever behavior is being offered, even if means building on something as small as a glance or a head turn. It's easy to fall into the trap of believing the dog is doing nothing but sitting and staring. In the beginning, click everything that isn't sitting and staring—a sigh, an ear flick, a glance away, a weight shift, etc. Start with what you're getting, even if it's just ear flicks and weight shifts, and build to something more. These first few training periods may not lead to a behavior you particularly want to work on again, but you will have accomplished a lot in terms of teaching your dog to actively participate in the process.

• *Brush up on your skills.* If you're a beginner yourself, your skills may be less than perfect, which can confuse or frustrate your dog. Practice your timing, make sure you're maintaining a high rate of reinforcement, and be certain your initial criterion is clear and achievable.

• *Be patient.* Especially if you have experience with "pure" clicker-trained dogs, it's easy to get frustrated with a crossover dog's reluctance to experiment. Realize that the modeling and luring (and corrections) used extensively in non-clicker methods teach a dog to wait to be shown what to do. You've changed the rules, and it will take time for your dog to learn them.

Food for Thought

I think one problem many motivated people run into early in trying to clicker train is trying to play the "101 Things..." game. I've concluded that this game is actually better suited for a more clicker-savvy dog. Once the dog understands the clicker-training process, the game is a wonderful tool, but before that, the game is often frustrating and confusing. When I tried it too early, I felt stupid and clumsy and my dog was more confused than anything else. It was a bit demoralizing! I suggest that people wait until they've taught the dog several behaviors and are comfortable and fluent using the clicker, before trying to play the "101 Things" game.

Greta L. Kaplan, Berkeley, CA

How do I shape a complex behavior, such as a fast, straight, square sit?

"Fast," "straight," and "square" are individual elements of a competition-quality sit. There are other elements too, such as "tucked," "lasting until released," "in position relative to the handler," and "in the presence of other dogs." It takes all of those elements—and others—to add up to a fully-trained, competition-quality sit.

A trainer's very first step, then, is to comprehensively define the finished behavior—breaking it into its components and preparing for the situation in which it will be done. Let's look at a complete list for the competition sit. It must be:

• tucked

• square

• straight

• immediate upon cue

• assumed from a stand or a down

• held in position until the dog is released (several minutes) even if the handler leaves

• done in any position relative to the handler (at heel, in front, at a distance)

• performed in any location, indoors and outdoors, on a variety of surfaces

• reliable in the presence of lots of other people (no matter what those people are doing)

• reliable in the presence of other dogs (no matter what those dogs are doing)

- reliable in the presence of food on the ground and all of the variety of smells and sounds associated with a dog show

Although the list looks long, it's in the trainer's best interest to be as exhaustive as possible. The more detailed you make your plan in the beginning, the less likely you are to run into a situation later that your dog is completely unprepared for.

Once you have your list of elements, you train for them, one element at a time, building each bit on top of the one that came before. Break each element down and teach it incrementally, luring, capturing, or shaping to get the initial behavior.

As a general rule of thumb, shape the elements of the behavior itself first. Once the behavior is perfect, add the cue. Then begin to train for other elements, such as distance, duration, generalization to multiple locations, and proofing against distractions.

Success Story

I had been trying to teach Roxy how to roll over for about two months. I did this by luring—asking her to lie down then holding a treat near her shoulder and coaxing her over, all the time saying "roll over." But she just didn't seem to get it. Then we discovered clicker training, and once she was over her initial fear of the sound and realized it meant Pork Liver Treats, she very quickly did everything she could to earn her treats and was so much fun to train.

Then one day I thought of roll over. I did exactly what I had done before—got her to lie down, lured her over with the treat, and gave the verbal cue—only this time, when her other side touched the floor, I clicked her as well. Do I really need to tell you what happened next? I asked her to roll over again, and she flopped down and whizzed over as though she had been doing it all her life! It just took the clicker to mark the end of the behavior so that she knew EXACTLY what "roll over" meant. I achieved in five seconds what I had been trying to teach for two months!

Val Leslie, Sydney, Australia

How do I train a chain of behaviors, such as a formal retrieve?

A competition retrieve isn't a single behavior. It's a compilation—a chain—of individual behaviors.

see also

What's the Premack principle?
page 190

In competition obedience, the retrieve begins with the dog sitting at the handler's side. The handler tosses the dumbbell and then cues the dog to get it; the dog retrieves the dumbbell and returns to a sit in front of the handler; on cue, the dog gives the dumbbell to the handler; then, on another cue, the dog returns to heel position.

To teach a behavior chain, you need to break the chain into its individual parts, train the individual parts separately, and then string them together. One particularly effective way of chaining is to start with the behaviors at the end of the chain and work backwards. This technique, called back-chaining, is effective because as the dog works its way through the chain, the behaviors are getting more and more familiar, and doing a familiar behavior actually serves as a reinforcer.

Keep these tips in mind when working with chains of behavior:

• Resist the urge to chain early. Get the individual parts strong and perfect first. If individual behaviors begin to fall apart within the chain, you chained too soon.

• Fade the clicker before chaining. If you still need the clicker to mark correct behavior, it's too soon to chain.

• Because each behavior in a chain reinforces the behavior that came before it, stop the chain if any part is substandard. For example, if the dog breaks the sit-stay in order to retrieve the dumbbell before being sent, have someone pick up the dumbbell. Don't continue the exercise. Each behavior in a chain is the reward for performing the behavior that came before it. If the behavior doesn't deserve a reward, stop the chain.

• Practice the individual parts outside of the chain. This continued reinforcement can only strengthen your chain.

CHAPTER 9 Making the Behavior Perfect

How can I train a behavior
before I add the cue?

see also

What does "getting the behavior" mean?
page 76

Mursblat. *Mursblat!* Darn it, MURSBLAT!

I'm guessing you have absolutely no clue what "mursblat" means. If you and I speak the same language, I can explain what an unfamiliar word means. But what if you and I don't speak the same language? How can I teach you to mursblat? I can:

• model

• lure

• capture

• shape

Out of the blue, you hear a click and I give you some chocolate. Mmm. You like that. Then another click and I give you another chocolate. Then it happens again. You start to realize that you've been doing the same thing every time just before I give you chocolate. So you test your theory. Sure enough, when you do the behavior, I click and give you chocolate. Pretty soon, you're mursblatting all over the place, without ever having heard the word.

Since we don't speak the same language, chances are "mursblat" doesn't stand out among the sea of other unintelligible sounds I make. But now, as you offer this behavior over and over, you start to notice that I'm saying "mursblat" every time you do it. Then there's the click and the treat. Once you make the connection, you test it. I say "mursblat" and you do what you think it means. Click! Jackpot! Communication achieved.

When and how do I add the cue?

In clicker training, we add the cue after the behavior is shaped and strong, not while the dog is learning it. Why?

For two reasons: First, when the pup is learning the behavior, we want him to concentrate on the behavior. At that point, the cue is meaningless to him anyway—just another bit of "noise" to sort through. In the beginning, make learning easier on your dog by minimizing distractions, including meaningless cue words. Second, we want the cue to be associated with the final, perfect form of the behavior. If you add the cue in the beginning, you run the risk of having an unfinished version of the behavior crop up when you least want it to—like during the stress of competition—even though you continued to shape a more precise behavior.

First get the behavior you want in the form you want it. One of the myths about clicker training is that we go around with a myriad of uncued behaviors for ages and ages. This is just that—a myth. Add the cue as soon as the dog is actively offering the behavior you want. For a simple behavior that could happen on the first day!

More complex behaviors may take more time to shape. If the behavior is extremely complex—a behavior chain, for example—you can add cues to the individual parts of the chain, and then add a cue for the entire chain when it's complete. Or, if the behavior is a single but very elaborate behavior, you can use temporary cues as you shape it, replacing them with a permanent cue when you've achieved its final form.

Once you have the behavior you want, practice it until the dog is actively offering exactly that behavior—that perfect behavior—eighty percent of the time, then add the cue. Remember, we're just looking for the behavior itself at this point. You'll train elements such as distance, duration, generalization to multiple locations, and proof against distractions after the behavior is on cue.

My dog is responding slowly to the cue. How can I get a faster response? **page 96**

see also

There are three kinds of cues: verbal cues, hand signals, and contextual cues. Contextual cues are environmental stimuli or situations that elicit the behavior. For example, the rattle of the dog's dish cues the dog to come for dinner. When heeling, a stop cues the dog to sit. Through training, the sight of a person approaching might become the cue for the dog to sit for petting.

In the beginning, a verbal cue or hand signal is meaningless to your dog. It is just one sight or sound in a sea of sights and sounds. Most of the sights and sounds—or stimuli—will remain meaningless, at least as far as the behavior you're training for goes. But as he performs the behavior, stimuli that remain constant begin to stand out. Before a cue can be used to elicit a behavior, it must first stand out—it must first be associated with the behavior. Here's how to make that happen:

1. Say the cue as the dog performs the behavior, immediately preceding the click. Repeat approximately fifty times.

2. Say the cue a little bit earlier—just as the dog begins to do the behavior. Repeat approximately fifty times.

3. Say the cue earlier still—just as the dog decides to do the behavior. Use your powers of observation to see that moment he commits himself. Repeat approximately fifty times.

In all these repetitions you haven't yet used the cue to elicit the behavior. All you've done is associate it with the dog's offered performance. Now it's time to begin using it to cause the behavior to happen.

When adding a cue, keep the following things in mind:

• Make sure nothing in the environment except your cue is consistent during your reps. This includes your hand/arm position, your body position, your position relative to the dog, distance from the dog, angle to you or relative to other things, and position in a room or environment.

• Verbal cues are incredibly difficult for a dog. We chatter at each other and at them all day, and to them our words flow together seamlessly. They simply don't have that kind of language, so listening for a particular sound in a sea of similar sounds is hard at best. What's more, dogs are incredibly good at subtle body signals—signals you're not even aware you're giving. Therefore, you must consciously work to be certain the cue you intend to add is the only consistent, salient stimulus.

- Once you begin using the cue to elicit the behavior, *stop reinforcing uncued performances of the behavior.* If the dog can simply offer the behavior and earn the reinforcement, why would he bother learning the cue? He can just run through his repertoire!

- In the beginning, the dog's response to the cue will probably be slow because he's still learning what it means. That's all right. After the dog is reliably responding to the cue, you can work on shortening the latency—the amount of time between the cue and the response.

- When you think the cue is strong, proof it. Vary the time between giving the cue and don't reinforce anticipated responses. Mix "nonsense" cues in with the real cue, and reinforce only the correct response to the real cue. Be careful not to fall into patterns when playing these games—dogs are quick to learn patterns.

- If your dog has two or more behaviors on cue, ask for different ones in a single session, reinforcing for the right response to the right cue.

> "
> When I first started, the stumbling block I remember most was the command-based way of thinking. I didn't see how the dog would know what to do if I didn't tell her first. It was a long time before someone pointed out to me that dogs don't automatically understand English, so there was no use telling them anyway!
>
> Wendy S. Katz, Lexington, KY
> "

My dog is responding slowly to the cue. How can I get a faster response?

Latency is the time between the cue and the response. Ideally, that time is zero—or as close to it as possible. Latency, as trainer Morgan Spector says, is habitual. If you make a short latency a requirement of every behavior you teach, the dog will automatically apply that concept to new behaviors.

Before you concentrate on shortening latency, proof the cue thoroughly. Until the dog is very sure what the cue means, it will take him time to "translate" it.

Once the cue is solidly attached, speed of response can be shaped like any other element:

- Determine your starting point by doing ten reps of the behavior and recording how long it takes for the dog to perform the behavior after you give the cue each time. Two seconds? Three? Eight? Add up the numbers you've recorded and divide by ten. The resulting average is your baseline—your starting point.

- Do ten reps, using your baseline as your criterion. Reinforce all responses that occur at or more quickly than your baseline. Consider all reps that take longer than your baseline as errors and do not reinforce them.

- At the end of ten reps, evaluate. If the dog got at least eight correct—made two or fewer errors—then you're ready to make it harder. If he made three or more errors, stay at this level during the next session. It may take several sessions to achieve eighty percent reliability.

- When you're ready to make it harder, cut the time by a second or so. Instead of doing the behavior within four seconds, the dog would be required to perform in three seconds in order to earn reinforcement.

- As you get closer to zero, you may need to tighten your criterion by only half a second in order for the dog to remain successful.

If your dog makes more than fifty percent incorrect responses in three consecutive sessions, reevaluate your latency criterion. You've moved too quickly.

When and how do I fade the clicker?

The clicker is a powerful marker signal, so reserve it for the early stages of training, when you need a marker to identify the correct behavior. Once the behavior is strongly on cue, replace the use of the clicker with a release word.

The release word functions in essentially the same way as the click, but it's less precise. Once you've shaped exactly the behavior you need, and put it on cue, you no longer need the precision of the clicker to identify the behavior you're working on.

Don't stop reinforcing the behavior, when you replace the clicker. Do, however, begin treating with reinforcers other than food treats sometimes.

Since you've replaced the clicker, does that mean you're just about done with training? Probably not. You probably still need to add elements such as duration, distance, proofing against distractions, and generalization to multiple locations.

see also

What can I use to reinforce my dog? **page 28**

How do I move from food treats to praise only? **page 37**

When and how do I add the cue? **page 93**

How do I add duration to a behavior? **page 98**

How do I add distance to a behavior? **page 100**

How do I train against distractions? **page 101**

How do I generalize to different locations and situations? **page 103**

How do I add duration to a behavior?

Some behaviors last only as long as it takes to perform the basic act. "Come" lasts until the dog gets to you. "Fetch" lasts until she returns with the object. Other "duration" behaviors have no set end point. "Sit" means remain sitting until told otherwise. The most common duration behaviors are sit, down, and walk on a loose leash.

Initially, teach duration by delaying the click (or release word). Start slow—with a delay of one second or one step—and gradually increase your duration criterion:

1. Ask for the behavior, and instead of clicking at the moment the dog does the behavior, wait one second before marking and reinforcing.

2. Repeat this procedure for one training session. Count the number of successful and unsuccessful repetitions.

3. At the end of the session, evaluate. If the dog met your criterion at least eighty percent of the time, increase your criterion by one or two seconds next time. If the dog was not successful eighty percent of the time, remain at the same criteria for the next session.

Repeat these three steps until the dog is able to perform the behavior for ten seconds. At this point, begin to reinforce your dog for doing the behavior for both shorter and longer periods of time within a given range:

1. Set a mid-range criterion. For example, twelve seconds if your dog reliably does the behavior for ten.

2. Divide your criterion by two (12 ÷ 2 = 6). Add the result to your criterion to get the upper limit to your range (12 + 6 = 18) and subtract it from your criterion to get the lower limit (12 − 6 = 6).

3. Do either five or ten reps per session, and plan ahead by choosing an equal number of values from the top and bottom halves of your range. In this example, I might choose to do five reps and plan to reinforce once after six seconds, once after twelve, once after eighteen, nine, and fifteen.

4. Randomize the values, so it's not predictable whether the dog will be doing a longer or shorter repetition.

5. Track the error percentage and use that information to pace future extensions of the time range.

The formula suggested above should work well as you increase duration by setting the mid-point of your range progressively higher and higher, but it's not set in stone. Continue to reinforce your dog for doing the behavior for only a short time in a real-life situation when that's appropriate.

If the behavior has a particular duration requirement, train at least fifty percent beyond it. For example, if you must have a three-minute sit in competition obedience, train until you have a reliable sit for at least four and a half minutes.

Once you achieve the maximum duration you desire, be unpredictable with regard to that element of the behavior. Dogs are quick to learn patterns. You want your dog to perform regardless of the duration of the individual repetition. Including a few short, easy reps during training will help pique the dog's interest.

When first working on the element of duration, stick strictly to that— don't try to add distance at the same time. Keep training as clear as possible by training one new element at a time. After the dog is reliably performing the behavior for an extended period of time, you can make it harder by adding the dimension of distance.

How do I add distance to a behavior?

see also

Should I keep records? **page 70**

How do I add duration to a behavior?
page 98

You ask your dog to sit while you walk back and forth from the car to the kitchen bringing in the groceries. You signal your off-leash dog, who's playing on a trail fifty feet ahead of you, to lie down until a group of hikers walks past. You send your field retriever to retrieve a bird that fell a quarter of a mile away.

All of these are examples of behaviors at distance. As with duration, the secrets to distance are slow, incremental progress in the learning phase and variability when maintaining the behavior.

Note: If the behavior also has duration, train duration first.

When you begin to work on distance, begin at a level at which you know the dog can be successful. A frequent complaint at the outset is "I can't get two feet away!" So don't start at two feet; start at one foot, or six inches, or just by shifting your weight backwards.

When you want the behavior to occur away from you in the first place— for example, a down at a distance—you may have to start by asking for it from just a few inches further away than usual, especially if the dog has gotten a high rate of reinforcement for doing it close to you in the past. You might help your dog grasp the concept of performing the behavior at a distance by capturing natural occurrences at a distance, or by using temporary barriers to prevent her from approaching you.

As you make the behavior more difficult by adding distractions or new criteria with more complex requirements, cut your distance temporarily. Shorter distances enable you to control your training during the learning phase, so you can concentrate on a single criterion. Shorter distances also let you do many more reps in the same amount of time.

Don't be in a hurry to increase distance. Get the other elements solid first. Distance is easy to add later.

How do I train against distractions?

A common complaint in any reinforcement training is "I can't offer anything as reinforcement that my dog wants more than squirrels/other people/other dogs/traffic/other distractions." That's probably true. If your dog is distracted by something, it's clearly the most reinforcing thing in the environment at that moment.

As often as possible, use the opportunity to interact with the distraction as reinforcement for desired behavior. In addition, desensitize your dog to the distraction, so he is able to maintain his concentration.

Desensitization is a process of exposing your dog to low levels of a stimulus, then gradually increasing the stimulus level as the dog's tolerance increases. To desensitize, set the level of exposure to the stimulus to the point where the dog is showing signs of arousal but is still able to focus and take treats. When the dog physically relaxes and is able to perform reliably at that level, increase the level of the stimulus.

Say, for example, that your dog loves other people and desperately wants to be petted by everyone he sees. To teach him to work in the presence of other people you might go to a parking lot. In the distance, you and your dog can see people walking in and out of a store. Get far enough away that your dog notices the people but isn't particularly concerned with them. Wait for him to relax, clicking and treating for attention to you. Then ask for a few well-known behaviors. When he is relaxed and focused, you can move a few feet closer to the people—just far enough that he again takes notice of them.

Distractions can be exciting, but they can also be frightening. If the stimulus is frightening, it's crucial to desensitize so gradually that you are simultaneously *counter-conditioning* the dog's emotional reaction.

see also

What if I can't offer a food treat or if my dog isn't interested in the reward I'm offering? **page 33**

Should I keep records? **page 70**

How can I get my dog to pay attention to me even in a distracting environment? **page 120**

How do I handle fearful behavior? **page 136**

What's the Premack principle? **page 190**

Counter-conditioning is the process of changing an emotional reaction by associating low levels of a scary or otherwise negative stimulus to higher levels of a powerful positive stimulus, such as food.

When desensitizing to a stimulus, you should never, ever increase the level of the stimulus enough to trigger an undesirable reaction — *especially if the dog is afraid of or aggressive toward the stimulus.* If the dog is pushed to the point where he is too distracted to work or too stressed to take treats, he is not benefiting from the experience. In the above example, if a person were to walk toward you in the parking lot where you're working, you could simply turn and walk the dog away as soon as she began to exhibit signs of excitement or stress.

How do I generalize
to different locations and situations?

Train in them!

"New and different" is always distracting and exciting. If you want your dog to perform reliably and calmly in any situation, train him in as many locations as possible—especially, but not exclusively, in the situations he'll be required to perform in.

Dogs don't generalize the way we do. If you teach sit in the kitchen next to the sink, the dog will likely learn that "sit" means sit in the kitchen next to the sink. He might not even generalize to other parts of the kitchen! If you do all your repetitions while you're standing up, with him positioned directly in front of you, he might further come to believe that "sit" should happen only when you're standing and he's in front of you.

The key to generalizing a concept is variability. Unless you want a particular something in the environment to become a cue for the behavior, you should make sure no irrelevant "somethings" remain constant as you train.

Should I keep records? **page 70**

see also

- Change your body position regularly—even with every repetition. Bend, sit, stretch, lie down, move your hands around, stand on one foot, do yoga poses.

- Change locations frequently. In the beginning, you'll have to train the behavior from scratch in each location. However, as you train in more and more locations, the dog will begin to generalize the behavior.

- Change your position within the environment. Train in different parts of the room, yard, or other location. Change the direction you face. Train at an angle to walls, furniture, or other straight lines.

- Unless the behavior is supposed to happen with the dog in a specific position relative to you—such as a sit in heel position or a straight "front"—change your relative positions. Cue behaviors when you are at an angle to, beside, in front of, and behind the dog. Teach your dog not to change his position before responding unless changing his position is part of the behavior.

Success Story

When I got my puppy, Borias, I really boned up on articles, books, and videos and was determined to raise my first clicker-trained dog. I am training him to be my service dog, in addition to agility, obedience, and companion. The first service-dog task I set out to teach was retrieving objects that I drop. So I decided, since many service dog trainees hate picking up metal objects, to use my keys. I started off by dropping them and saying "Get it!" in a fun way, giving a cue we used for picking up his toys. I clicked for mouthing [the keys] and little pick-ups, and then I'd put my hand out to catch them as they dropped, making a huge deal saying an emphatic "thank you!" which he seemed to just love. He was hooked. In one session, he knew what I wanted!

I hadn't worked on it in several weeks, as we had moved to many other things, puppy brains being the sponges they are.

When Borias was fourteen weeks old, I was working on being with me in grocery stores. I was going down an aisle, picking out stuff with a basket on my lap, when I suddenly noticed my wallet was no longer on my lap. I said, "Oh no, my wallet. Where's my wallet?" Borias turned around and lunged at something. In his mouth was my little red wallet, which he bounced back and put right in my hand! Of course, he got many hugs and kisses and thank-yous as he wiggled with glee.

He's quite helpful with things like that. Sometimes my shoe will fall off when transferring to my wheelchair, and before I can even ask, he's got it and given it to me. Another favorite job is to take my socks off for me—something mischievous that came naturally that I turned into a "job." He loves his work.

Tamandra Michaels, Los Angeles, CA

CHAPTER **10** Reliability and Fluency

Are clicker-trained behaviors reliable?

Reliability is a number. It's a percentage of successful trials. No matter what training method you use, reliability is obtained through repetition. Clicker-trained behaviors are as reliable as the trainer is willing to work to make them be.

see also

Should I keep records? **page 70**

What is "fluent," and how do I get there? **page 112**

B.F. Skinner, a pioneer in behavioral research, defined the principles of operant conditioning in the 1930s, and two of his graduate students, Keller and Marian Breland, took the technology out of the laboratory and put it to commercial use. During its forty-seven year history, their business, called Animal Behavior Enterprises, trained fifteen thousand animals of over a hundred and forty different species, including dogs.

Many of those animals were for "automated" exhibits at fairs—"play tic tac toe against the chicken"—and for elaborate all-animal stage shows. However, not all of their work was commercial. Much of it was for the government. Beginning with WWII through most of the Cold War, the Brelands took on lots of interesting challenges:

- They trained pigeons to go ahead of military troops to search for ambushes in the jungle.

- They trained ravens to fly into enemy territory at night, guided by a laser, and once at the correct building to take pictures using tiny cameras hung around their necks and then return.

- They trained wild-caught adult dolphins to do open-water work. Some of the tasks the animals performed required them to work away from the boat for eight or more hours at a time.

- They trained dogs to detect mines and trip-wires in war zones and, more importantly, to prevent soldiers from tripping them.

Distance work was a given. Birds flew free for hours and searched hundreds of square miles of ocean. Dolphins swam—alone—up to four hours away from their trainers and four hours back. Cats were guided from great distances by sound only.

Whether the project was commercial or done for the government, the Brelands, and later the Baileys, required reliability. Not kind of reliable. Not even most-of-the-time reliable. Reliable. They weren't going for scores or a ribbon. There were, in many cases quite literally, human lives depending on the reliability of these animals' behavior.

And the method they used was operant conditioning. They used positive reinforcement, extinction, and occasionally negative punishment (the withdrawal of something the animal desires). They used positive punishment (aversives) only about a dozen times in fifty years—and those were at the request of the client.

Although the Brelands were leaders in the fight for humane treatment of captive animals, they didn't choose this method because it felt good; they chose it because it gave them the results they needed in the fastest time. They experimented to find the best way. Trial and error. But most importantly, they kept *data*—gobs and gobs of scientific data—and based their programs on what it showed. They didn't rush their animals or put them to work until the data demonstrated that the behavior was as reliable as it needed to be—whether that meant one error in a hundred trials or one in ten thousand.

All this cookie training is great,
but how do I teach my dog there are some instances where he has no choice?

see also

What do I do if my dog intentionally disobeys a known command?
page 55

Should I keep records? **page 70**

My dog is responding slowly to the cue. How can I get a faster response?
page 96

What is "fluent," and how do I get there? **page 112**

You can't, because he always has a choice; unless you are physically manipulating him, it's the dog who determines what he will or won't do.

What you want is a behavior with short latency (meaning it occurs as soon as the cue is given) and high reliability. Latency is an element that can be trained like any other element. Again, reliability is a number. Data. Cold data with no relation to "dominance" or "control." Reliability is obtained through reinforced repetition.

I've been driving cars with manual transmissions for close to fifteen years. Over that time, I've had an incredible number of reinforced repetitions (meaning the car did what I wanted it to do) for using the clutch properly.

I remember learning how to do it. It was hard, because I'm not terribly coordinated. Shifting once the car was moving wasn't too difficult, but getting started from a stop was murder. So I and my "trainer" did lots of reps. We started in a parking lot—no distractions, few restrictions. When my reliability improved, we "raised the criteria" and went to a neighborhood street. I was back at square one in that environment, but through practice I improved. Then we went to more populated streets. Whoa—drop in performance once again! But again I quickly improved. Gradually we added hills. We added the pressure of cars behind me at a stoplight at a busy intersection. I had *thousands* of repetitions before I got relatively good at getting that car started smoothly.

For a very long time, using the clutch was a deliberate, conscious behavior. I had to think about it every time. Over time that changed, and I don't usually think about it anymore. I don't have to. I'm *fluent* in the behavior. Latency is immediate. Reliability is nearly 100 percent.

Nearly. Once in a blue moon I still stall the car. It happens. I'm not perfect, even after almost fifteen years' worth of repetitions.

And yet the behavior is under my control. I can choose not to use the clutch anytime I want to. I can pop the clutch intentionally. Never, never, never will that behavior be out of my control.

If you want your dog's behavior to be as reliable as my "get the manual transmission car moving" behavior is, there's only one way to do it. Practice with intent. Generalize the behavior. Practice under the conditions in which you need the behavior to be reliable. Work on latency. Reinforce the behavior so strongly that the dog does want to do it.

You determine which cues are and reinforcers to use and train for immediate responses by rewarding them, but never fool yourself into thinking training overcomes free will.

I don't simply want to participate—
I want to win! Are clicker-trained behaviors precise enough and reliable enough for competition?

see also

I'm interested in canine sports. Can a dog be clicker trained for activities such as agility, tracking, competition obedience, flyball, or Schutzhund?
page 6

Clicker-trained behaviors can be both precise and reliable.

How precise? The clicker has been likened to a surgeon's scalpel, enabling a trainer to isolate and train the tiniest of behaviors. Examples include head position, ear position, tail position. Imagine what a wonderful impression a dog would make in the conformation ring if she were trained not only to gait and stack, but also to prick up her ears, make eye contact, and wag her tail when the judge comes by!

How reliable? Clicker trainers define reliability in terms of the percentage of successful responses. It's the trainer's responsibility to set a goal for reliability in a certain environment and then to train in that environment, keeping records, until your data shows that you have achieved your goal.

However, clicker-trained behaviors will be neither precise nor reliable if you're not skilled enough to train to the level you desire. As Bob Bailey is fond of saying, based on years of experience, clicker training is simple, but it isn't always easy. It takes practice and it takes work. You need:

• Motivation to study, learn, and work hard

• Resources to learn the ins and outs of the sport in which you're interested

• Willingness to practice, keep records, and constantly, objectively, assess your training plan

• Time to devote to training and a dog that is both physically and mentally suited to the job you've chosen for it

If you have all these elements, then clicker training is the most precise and reliable method of making your dog a winner.

You say I can do competition obedience,
but I can't use a clicker or food in the ring.
How can I clicker train?

Let's look at these two aspects of clicker training separately.

The clicker is an event marker. Once you've trained the behavior you want, you no longer need to use a tool as precise as the clicker to mark it. At that point you can fade the clicker and replace it with a release word.

Food is just one of the reinforcers available to you. It's a great reinforcer—small, easy to deliver, and extremely powerful. For those reasons I encourage people to use it frequently in training. However, when it comes time for the actual performance, you can't use food and yet you don't want to confuse your dog with a sudden change. So what do you do?

First, condition a reinforcer you can use in the ring. A behavior the dog enjoys doing can be used as a reinforcer for another behavior. You're allowed to praise and celebrate a bit between exercises as long as your dog remains "under control." Develop a fun "happy dance" that you and your dog can de-stress with. Have your dog perform her favorite trick—especially if that trick makes the audience laugh. Laughter is incredibly reinforcing to many dogs. Use its reinforcing power to your own advantage! Once you discover a trick your dog adores doing, reserve it for special times—like at the end of a spectacularly performed obedience behavior.

Second, keep in mind that the only time you can't use food as reinforcement is in the ring during an actual trial. Compared to the number of times you practice these behaviors, that's a relatively minute number of repetitions. Don't rob yourself of a powerful reinforcer by phasing out food too soon or too quickly.

For more information on clicker training for obedience, refer to Morgan Spector's excellent book by that name.

see also

What can I use to reinforce my dog? **page 28**

How do I move from food treats to praise only? **page 37**

When and how do I fade the clicker? **page 97**

What is "fluent" and how do I get there?

A fluent behavior is defined as one that is accurate, reliable, and has a standardized rate of response in any situation. Let's look at the requirements within that definition one at a time:

- *In any situation.* A situation is more than a location. It's a complete environment, including all of its distractions. A dog that can perform the behavior in the park except when other dogs—or children, nearby traffic, or strong wind and rain—are present is not fluent (yet).

- *Accuracy.* The behavior should be exactly what you want. If the behavior is a competition-quality sit, it should be tucked, square, and straight. If you still get crooked sits, the behavior isn't accurate—or fluent.

- *Reliability.* The behavior should happen when you want. As the trainer, it's your responsibility to determine the desired level of reliability and train until the dog reaches that level in each situation. Until your data shows that the dog has reached that standard of reliability, the behavior is not fluent.

- *A standardized rate of response.* The dog should respond to the cue at a predictable rate. If the dog responds within one second most of the time but only after several seconds in the presence of some distractions, she is not fluent in that behavior. Train a short latency and make it a required element in every successful repetition during training.

Because dogs don't generalize well—"sit" in the kitchen is a completely different behavior than "sit" in the park—the task of training to fluency is complex, even daunting.

Steve White, a former police K9 trainer, used the "20-20-20 pyramid" to ensure his dogs were exceedingly fluent in their behaviors. For each behavior, he required twenty successful repetitions in twenty different locations with twenty different distractions.

However, very few trainers are willing to train to that level of fluency, nor is it necessary for most purposes. Usually we don't need every behavior to be fluent in every possible situation. And in fact some behaviors are contextual, meaning we look for them to occur only in very specific circumstances. For example, my dogs have been trained to stay out of our kitchen, but that behavior is specific to our kitchen—not kitchens in other houses and not other rooms in our house.

For most of us, a more realistic definition of fluency would be "a fluent behavior is one that is accurate, reliable, and has a standardized rate of response in a specific situation." As trainer, it's up to you to determine what "fluent" will mean for each of your dog's behaviors. Before you begin to train a behavior, ask yourself:

• What does a perfect performance look like?

• In what locations will my dog have to perform the behavior?

• What distractions might the dog face in each of these locations?

• How reliable must this behavior be *in each situation?*

• Do human lives—or the dog's—depend on the performance of this behavior?

• Is a significant amount of money invested in the performance of this behavior?

• Will performance of this behavior improve your dog's quality of life by, for example, enabling him to accompany you away from the house or simply making daily life more peaceful?

• Is this behavior "just for fun"?

• What's an acceptable latency? Must the behavior be immediate or is "soon" acceptable?

Once you answer each of these questions, use the answers to make a training plan and keep data to help you ensure that your dog reaches fluency in the necessary situations.

How long will it take to train my dog?

see also

At what point does my dog "know" what is being asked of him? **page 120**

"Training a dog," or even training a behavior, is not a matter of a certain number of repetitions or a specific length of time. Lots of factors influence how long the process takes:

• your dog's age and history

• your dog's genetic background

• your ability to set and evaluate criteria

• your timing and consistency

• the number of reinforced repetitions

• the quality of the reinforcers you use (context plays a role)

• the number of locations the behavior(s) must be fluent in

• the number of distractions that must be trained against

• the level of reliability required for each behavior

• the overall complexity of the behavior(s)

Furthermore, there will never be a day when you find you're miraculously finished training your dog. Learned behaviors need to be practiced and reinforced or they will be forgotten. Your dog will continue to learn for the rest of his life and if you stop teaching—stop managing your dog's environment and reinforcing desired behaviors only—he will teach himself other behaviors to get what he wants.

> Approach training with a sense of humor, and a relaxed, patient attitude. You will make mistakes, and that's okay. It's part of the learning process. Keep working to improve your skill and understanding, but don't lament mistakes—and don't give up! Remember that you may know exactly what you want your dog to do, but your dog hasn't a clue! Resist the urge to get impatient and frustrated with your dog (and yourself). Have fun!
>
> Terri Stilson, Seattle, WA

Success Story

My two-year-old Briard Ricochet is my first "from scratch" clicker trained dog. I come from a 25+ year background in Koehler-based compulsion training. I decided that this puppy would be my experiment in training without physical force. Well, it wasn't all smooth sailing by any means. Ricochet is a very high energy dog with lots of prey drive. She jumped on everyone, she loved to pounce at other dogs, and loose leash walking was a long time coming. There were many times when I was tempted to fall back on the methods that had been so successful for me in the past.

I persevered. I carried a clicker and treats everywhere we went. I took the time to have the deck stacked in our favor by being in control of all reinforcement. Ricochet wore a Gentle Leader for several months. We were early to every dog activity we attended so I could set the situation up for success. My friends (doggy and non) thought I was "obsessed" and "going overboard" when "one good pop would stop that nonsense." I confess there was more than once I thought I was wrong and I'd never have a controllable, mannerly dog.

Last weekend we showed in our fourth weekend agility trial. Aside from being very successful in the ring, Ricochet's behavior outside the ring was exemplary. She played tug and fetch off-leash with no interest in passing dogs. She waited quietly for her turn in the ring on a "settle" at my feet while maniacal border collies and yappy shelties milled around us. She walked to the start line on a loose leash and sat quietly as I walked out into the ring. At this large trial, she was the calmest and most polished novice dog there.

I guess I'm writing this to encourage those of you who have made the leap of faith that clicker training requires. It does work. Just hang in there and reward the positive and ignore the negative. Take the time to set yourself and your dog up for success and it will come.

Cathi Cline, Sacramento, CA

At what point does my dog "know" what is being asked of him?

see also

How do I know when to "make it harder"—increase my criteria for training? **page 80**

How do I generalize to different locations and situations? **page 103**

On the first night of each of my classes, I play "the training game" with my students, asking them to pair up and use the clicker to "train" each other, just to see how it works. It's a lot of fun. One of several things that always happens is that after someone has been clicked for performing the desired behavior, he or she says, "That was great! What did I do?"

That's a *hugely* important lesson for trainers. Just because you know what you're reinforcing doesn't mean the dog does, *even when the behavior is being freely offered*. (If you think this is mind-boggling in regards to desired behavior, now think about it in regards to undesired behavior. "He knows what he did wrong," people say of a dog. Are you sure?)

When you begin training a behavior, you may get the behavior before your dog consciously understands what you're reinforcing. Guess what? That's okay. At that level it's important only that you mark and reinforce behavior when it occurs. Then, when the dog achieves your initial criterion reliably, you can increase your requirements. Let your data guide you.

As you continue to train, you want to be certain you and your dog have the same understanding of what's being trained. It's very easy to believe you've trained one behavior, only to discover that when you change the environment you find your dog has interpreted it as something else entirely.

To help make sure you and your dog are on the same wavelength, teach the behavior from scratch in more than one way or in several locations. As the lesson is repeated, the dog will begin to generalize the behavior and figure out the underlying concept.

If my dog already knows a behavior, should I use the clicker?

see also

My dog doesn't seem to know what the clicker means except a treat is coming. How can I teach him the click is an event marker? **page 25**

Are you satisfied with the behavior?

If the behavior is on cue and you're generally satisfied with it, don't use the clicker. It would signify only that a treat is coming. The goal is for the clicker to become an event marker, not treat marker, and once the is learned and performed on cue, it's not conveying new info.

However, if you're not satisfied with the behavior the clicker is a great tool to use to make it better. You might even consider starting over and teaching the entire behavior from scratch using the clicker.

What is targeting, and why should I do it?

Targeting is touching a specified object with a nose, paw, or other body part. Touching one object can be generalized to touching other objects. This behavior is almost limitless in its applications. For example, targeting is the basic behavior underlying many other behaviors including:

• ringing a bell to ask to go outside

• pushing a door open or shut

• turning on or off a light (a common service-dog behavior)

• picking up an indicated object

A target can also be used as a lure. Instead of remaining stationary, the target—for example, your finger or the end of a stick—is used to lead the dog through the desired behavior. For example, a target stick held on the left side of your body can guide a dog into correct heel position. Similarly, the dog can follow the stick in a circle to learn a spin or to the ground to learn to lie down.

The target stick is used like a food lure, but it has an advantage over food. Often, as a dog follows a food lure he focuses so completely on the lure that he becomes unaware of anything else that is happening, including what his body is doing. A target stick is still a lure, but with a stick the dog is more likely to remain engaged in the task, making it easier to fade the lure later.

What does "getting the behavior" mean? **page 75**

see also

Targeting is an excellent behavior for both beginning clicker trainers and untrained or crossover dogs. It's a simple concept, and it's clear when to click. Plus, dogs seem to love it!

Teaching targeting is easy:

1. Choose your target and present it to the dog, just an inch or two from his nose. If the dog doesn't seem to notice the stick, you can rub a bit of cheese or hot dog juice on it to make it more interesting. The moment his nose touches the target, click and reinforce.

2. Repeat, with the target in the same place.

3. After five to ten repetitions with the target in that place, hold it at a different angle—still only an inch or two from his nose—and repeat the process.

4. Repeat the process with the target an inch or two in front of, above, below, to the left of, and to the right of the dog's nose.

5. Move the target out a couple of inches and repeat. Get at least five reinforced touches in each location (above, below, etc.).

6. Continue moving the target out, making sure the dog is performing reliably at each distance before increasing the criteria.

How can I get my dog to pay attention to me
even in a distracting environment?

One of the most common complaints I hear is "As soon as my dog and I walk out the door, I cease to exist. My dog is so distracted by all the sights, sounds, and events outside that I can't get his attention no matter what kind of treat I use."

The problem here isn't the quality of reinforcer (though of course that's important). The problem is that the dog hasn't learned to focus on you in distracting situations.

Focus, also known as attention, is a learned behavior. It must be taught step by step. It's the most important behavior you'll ever teach, because it's a pre-requisite to every other. If you can't get and maintain the dog's attention—especially in distracting situations—how can you get any other behavior? Your dog's very life may depend upon the strength of this basic behavior.

Attention doesn't have to mean eye contact. Indeed, the dog can be quite attuned to you without maintaining eye contact. However, eye contact is the start.

Teaching Eye Contact
Each step in the following progression describes one criterion. Do not progress to the next step until your dog is demonstrating reliability at the current one:

1. In the living room, kneel down with your dog. Hold an especially yummy treat in your fist and offer it to the dog. Allow the dog to sniff and lick and try to get the treat, but don't give it to him. The instant he pauses, click and offer the treat.

2. Repeat, this time clicking when the dog has ignored the treat for a full second.

3. Hold a yummy treat in your closed fist out away from your body. Wait until the dog glances at your face, then click. Even an eye flicker in your direction is enough.

4. Repeat the three steps above, this time in the kitchen.

5. Again in the kitchen, hold a treat away from your body, and this time, wait for half a second of eye contact before clicking.

   Note: Your dog may be uncomfortable offering eye contact. You may have to do a set of repetitions with just a quarter of a second of eye contact, then half a second. This is all right—eye contact is a matter of trust—but do not progress until your dog will hold eye contact for half a second.

6. Repeat the last step, clicking for a full second of eye contact.

Understand the sequence? Continue practicing, working up to several seconds of eye contact. Then add these criteria:

• different rooms in the house

• front yard and back yard

• waving the treat around

• another person nearby

• another person walking by

• another person waving his or her arms

Remember, every time you add a new criterion you may need to relax your duration requirement a bit until the dog learns that the rules are still the same.

Taking It on the Road

Attention at home is just a start. What you really need is the ability to get your dog's attention anywhere, anytime. Have you ever taken your dog on a trip to the park? She's so excited by all the new sights, sounds, and smells that you are completely forgotten. It's pretty certain you could wave raw steak under her nose, and she wouldn't respond.

The solution to this state of affairs is three-fold:

• Reduce "out–of–the–house" excitement with frequent trips. If you take a child to a circus once a year, she will be absorbed in the novelty of the experience. To try to get her to do math homework at the circus would be utter folly. Even if you found a spot and gave her the materials, she wouldn't be able to concentrate. Instead, math is done in the classroom or at home at the kitchen table, places so well known that she isn't distracted. On the other hand, the children of circus performers have grown up in the circus; they can do their homework there because they find the lights and sounds normal. If your dog gets out of the house only for the occasional trip to the vet or groomer, she's going to be so excited by the novelty of leaving home that ordinary things (like you!) are going to be ignored. On the other hand, with training, a dog who goes out regularly will react calmly to the plethora of stimuli.

• Teach your dog to focus on you in every situation. The natural inclination in new or exciting situations is to focus on the environment. You have to teach the dog to focus on you. You do this in much the same way that you taught her to make eye contact in the house. Start in a fairly boring location, reinforce the most minimal response, then gradually increase your criteria. Move closer to any distractions, but if they start to overwhelm, move away to the point the dog is able to concentrate. Then go to a new location and repeat the process. Then another. Then another. Build the habit of attention through repetition. If the dog doesn't get the opportunity to practice this skill, it will disappear.

• Teach your dog that you control her interactions with the environment. Although there are times when you need your dog to focus and ignore distractions, those times need to be balanced with opportunities to explore the environment—to sniff and mark, meet and greet. You can teach her to pay attention to you and to do what you want, but you must also meet her needs. She isn't a robot here to do your bidding. The best way to both meet your dog's needs and get the behavior you want is to make interacting with people and places contingent on her actions. Want to get out of the car? Sit and make eye contact with me first. Want to sniff that bush? Walk on a loose leash. Want to be petted by that stranger? Sit politely.

Finding the Balance

Sure, there are going to be times that your dog won't get to explore his environment. But it will be a lot easier to handle those times if they are balanced with times when he does. Rather than trying to teach your dog to ignore his surroundings, use the opportunity to explore them as reinforcement for a job well done.

1. *Go to a location away from your house.* Find a place low in distractions to start. An ideal location is one where interesting distractions are nearby but where you have the flexibility to move closer or further from them as necessary—such as the far end of a parking lot, say, or a quiet corner of a park.

2. *Get out of the car, dog on leash, and wait.* Give your dog only a foot or two of leeway on the leash to move around. Begin in a place where there's little of interest to the dog. It's important that he not be able to amuse himself.

3. *Wait.* Don't call the dog, pat your leg, make kissing noises, or do anything else to attract his attention—just wait.

4. *When the dog glances at you, click and treat.* Be certain to use a high-value reinforcer.

5. *Continue to wait and to reinforce glances toward you.* Be patient. Eventually your dog will decide you are the most interesting thing around, and will focus primarily on you. This could take ten minutes, or twenty, or even more! Patience is the key.

6. *After a series of reinforced reps, call it quits and do something that's fun for the dog.* Play a quick game of tug or simply walk him around on a loose leash, letting him sniff and look and explore. If you're at a park, you might be able to play fetch. If you're at the PETsMART parking lot, take a walk around the store.

7. *Repeat often over the next few weeks.* Help your dog generalize by moving closer to distractions in the same location and training in new ones After each session, reinforce attention by letting the dog interact with the environment.

Finally, attention is not something you'll train for and then forget about. This behavior needs to become part of your everyday routine. Every time you start a training session, start with attention. And even if you're not actively training for a new behavior, if you make attention a precursor to any and all interactions with your dog—especially outside the house—focusing on you will become a habit.

How do I train my dog to sit?

Training your dog to sit? How hard can that be? Just pop him a cookie for putting his butt on the ground—right?

Unfortunately, a *reliable* sit isn't quite that easy. Let's look first at how to get the behavior, then let's go over what it takes to get the behavior *when you want it, the way you want it.*

Getting the Behavior
A simple, "butt on the ground" sit is easy to get through either luring or capturing.

- *Luring*: To lure the sit from a stand, use a piece of food to draw your dog's nose up and back. As his head goes back, his rear end will naturally go down. Click at the moment his rear touches the ground, then let him have the treat.

- *Capture*: To capture the sit, simply wait until the dog sits down. Click at the instant his rear hits the ground and give him a treat right away.

If you're training for competition, a sit is more complex. It has additional requirements like "tucked," "square," and "straight." Each of those requirements is a criterion to be shaped.

Making It Perfect
Getting the sit is just the first step. Consider each of these questions:

- Do you want the sit cued with a verbal cue, a hand signal, or a contextual cue, i.e. every time you halt?

- How long should the sit last? Five seconds? Five minutes? Longer?

- Do you want the dog to hold the sit while you move around or will you always be stationary?

- Does sit mean "sit in front of me?" Or do you want the sit to happen no matter where the dog is—and no matter where you are?

- Where are you going to want the dog to sit? In the living room? The back yard? Away from home?

- What are some potential distractions that might occur when you want the dog to sit? Other people? Other dogs? Kids on skateboards? Squirrels?

- How reliable is this behavior going to need to be? Are a slow response and multiple cues irritating but acceptable, or could your dog's safety potentially depend on the reliability of this behavior?

As the trainer, it's up to you to figure out how and when you'll use the behavior and then to train for those occasions. Training sit in the kitchen and then expecting the dog to respond when off the leash at a dog park is utterly unrealistic—and utterly unfair to your dog.

No matter how you define sit—or any other behavior—for your dog, keep this progression in mind when you train:

- Get exactly the behavior you want.

- Add the cue.

- Make the behavior perfect by generalizing to different locations and adding elements such as duration, distance, and distractions.

- Make the behavior reliable by proofing everything you've taught in every situation you plan to use the behavior in.

> "
> Be consistent. When I was teaching Arden to sit by the road before we crossed, often she wouldn't, so I'd think, "Okay, next time..." But once I made the decision that We Are Not Crossing The Road Until Arden Sits Down, she picked it up almost immediately.
>
> Dr. Tracie Barber, Sydney, Australia
> "

How do I train my dog to lie down?

Various trainers have developed incredibly complex methods of compelling or luring a dog into lying down. However, the easiest way to teach a down is simply to capture it. Even the most frenetic dog will eventually settle and lie down. The trick is to make that behavior likely, so you have something to click and reinforce.

Getting the Behavior

The best place to start capturing the down is in a bathroom—it's small and easy to clear of all potential distractions. Take your dog in, shut the door, and wait. Sit down and read a magazine. Ignore your dog. Eventually, she will lie down. The moment she settles, click and offer a treat.

As soon as you click, your dog will probably become very interested in you. She'll sit in front of you, stare holes in you, and try any and every behavior you've ever reinforced.

Ignore her. Read your magazine. Eventually, she'll stop trying to entice you and lie down again. *Click!*

Do ten repetitions, then go play a game. Do another session later in the day or the next day. How long should you train in the bathroom? Keep doing bathroom sessions until the dog is actively offering downs to "make" you click. When you can get five downs in less than a minute you're probably ready to move to another room. It might take one session, or two, or ten.

Making It Perfect

Getting the down is just the first step. Next add a cue, establish reliability in different locations, train for duration and/or distance, etc. As the trainer, it's up to you to figure out how and when you'll use the behavior and then to train for those occasions. The questions listed previously, under "How do I train my dog to sit?" can help you formulate a plan.

Again, no matter how you define down—or any other behavior—for your dog, keep the same progression in mind when you train:

• Get exactly the behavior you want.

• Add the cue.

• Make the behavior perfect by generalizing to different locations and adding elements such as duration, distance, and distractions.

• Make the behavior reliable by proofing everything you've taught in every situation you plan to use the behavior in.

How do I train my dog to come when called?

A recall can save your dog's life. It can stop her from running in front of a car, or from chasing an animal into the woods. It can call your dog away from a tempting but dangerous delicacy she has just discovered.

Getting the Behavior

Teaching a recall is easy—just reinforce your dog for coming to you! Start by kneeling a few feet away and making happy noises. Click when the pup takes her first step toward you and give her a yummy treat when she gets to you. Run a few feet away and repeat the process. Make it a fun game! When she's reliably coming to you, start using your cue.

Add distance and distractions to the recall just as you would for a sit or other behavior. Calling a young puppy from across the yard when she is exploring a new, interesting scent is setting yourself and your pup up to fail. Walk to within a few feet, kneel down, and call her from there—and make sure to reinforce her for abandoning the distraction with something even better.

Success comes from repetition. Don't increase your distance or distractions until your dog responds immediately and enthusiastically to the recall cue. While you're training, remember to give a super-good reinforcement *every* time you call your dog.

The Collar Grab

When you call your dog, take hold of her collar before you deliver the reinforcer—and do that every single time. It does you no good to have a recall if you can't then catch your dog, and dogs have been killed because they avoided their owners' hands and at the last moment bolted into the street.

Having someone reach out to grab and restrain you is startling at best. Associate reaching and grabbing with good things by feeding a yummy treat once you have a hand on your pet's collar.

Exercises for Excellence

Try these recall games to help teach your pet recalls are fun and rewarding:

- When your dog is several feet away, say her name and give your recall cue. Then begin running backwards away from the dog. Click when she starts toward you and reward her when she catches up. This exercise engages the dog's natural desire to chase.

- Ask one or more friends or family members to help. Stand eight or ten feet apart, facing each other (or make a circle, if you have more than two people). Have one person call the dog. Click as soon as she starts toward the person, and have the person give a treat. Then have the next person call her. Repeat, gradually increasing the distance between people.

- Practice recalls in your house. Call your dog from across the room, from another room, from upstairs, from downstairs. Have a friend hold your dog (or ask your dog to stay) for a moment, then play hide and seek.

Tips for Success

Keep the following tips in mind as you train your recall and incorporate the recall into everyday life:

- *Always* make recalls rewarding.

- Use the highest value rewards you have.

- If you don't have a reward handy, make a big production of taking your dog to get one. She earned it, and the whole party is a jackpot.

- Practice calling your dog away from something she wants, give her a high-value reward, and then *let her go back to what she was doing*. Practice that a lot.

- Do lots and lots of short-distance recalls. You'll get more reps and build a habit faster.

Success Story

Yesterday we had two cable guys trying to fix our connections. I had put Bo, our year-old male Labrador, in the backyard. The guys went into the backyard and proceeded to let Bo into the kitchen, through the kitchen gate, and out the front door. I heard some yelling so I went to investigate, and there was Bo across the street with the guys calling and chasing him. He was having a grand time! I took and deep breath, prayed it would work, and yelled "Bo, here!" He looked up and came tearing toward me, right into the house! I was soooo proud of him! The guys were amazed. They wanted to know how I managed that since they both had dogs that wouldn't come when called. I explained the principles and how it must be trained consistently and in increasing distractions. I then fed Bo lots of big chunks of left over T-bone steak. He was in heaven and so was I.

Peggy Schaefer, Houston, TX

- Grab your dog's collar before you give the reward every time. Again, a recall is no good if you can't catch your dog.

- Call your dog one time. If she doesn't respond, go and get her (except during training, when a non-response is considered an error and dealt with through extinction).

- Don't call your dog when she isn't going to respond. Yelling "Missy, come!" over and over as she runs around ignoring you only weakens your cue.

- Practice your recall in distracting situations, increasing the level of distractions gradually.

Finally, *don't* take recalls for granted. Remember, your dog's life could depend on the reliability of her response. This means *never, ever punish a recall:*

- Don't call your dog and then do something she doesn't like, such as crating or confining her and then leaving her alone.

- If your dog is doing something you don't want her to do, don't call her and scold her—or even call her and ignore her. If you call her, reinforce her for coming.

- If your dog is doing something she enjoys, don't call her away without rewarding her. Balance the times when fun ends with several "practice" recalls after which she is allowed to go back to what she was doing.

How do I train my dog to walk on a loose leash?

Loose leash walking is one of the most challenging behaviors to teach. It's not a particularly "natural" behavior—there's no equivalent in the dog world—and walking relative to something else is a non-discrete behavior, which means that there's no obvious "right" or "wrong"—the trainer decides what's acceptable. So it's tough on the dog and tough on the trainer.

That said, it *is* possible to teach your dog to walk nicely with you without pulling on the leash. However, to be completely fair—and to give yourself (and your dog) the highest probability of success—you need to look at the whole picture, and consider the dog's wants and needs as well as your own agenda.

Taking Your Dog's Age into Account

To begin with, how old is the dog you're training? Adjusting your methods and expectations in accordance with your dog's developmental needs will help ensure success.

Puppies (0 to six months of age): Puppies are brand new to the world. Literally. Everything is new to them. They have little or no history—good or bad—related to what you want. A puppy also has a very short span of attention.

With puppies, paying attention to you and taking a few steps on a loose leash should be highly reinforced *and* followed by a lot of playing/sniffing/exploring. Then a few more exciting, highly reinforced steps followed by more playing/sniffing/exploring. Think of it as "on" and "off"—and have cues for each, such as "with me" and "go play."

This freedom to play and explore isn't a gift you're giving your dog. It's necessary. Your puppy must learn about the world around him. It's part

How do I add distance to a behavior? **page 98**

How do I train against distractions? **page 101**

How do I generalize to different locations and situations? **page 103**

How can I get my dog to pay attention to me even in a distracting environment? **page 120**

see also

of his development and socialization. If he doesn't experience lots of things at this critical time, he's likely to be fearful and insecure later.

Adolescents (six months to three years): Your dog may look like an adult, and you may feel like he's been around forever and "should act better," but if he's under three you've got an adolescent on your hands.

Adolescence is a time of boundless energy. It's the time when your dog grows up mentally—when he begins testing all of the choices available to him and making decisions about which path he's going to follow. This isn't rebellion. It's not stubbornness or defiance or dominance. It's nature's way of preparing the animal for the time when his caretakers won't be there to protect him. "Because I said so" doesn't cut it anymore. He has to find out for himself what works and what doesn't.

This is a challenging age. Your dog is bigger and stronger, and he's full of energy. Now, more than at any other time, you need to be consistent. Remember, every time you give in and let him pull on the leash, you're not only reinforcing pulling, you're putting this behavior on a variable schedule of reinforcement and thus *strengthening* it.

When you need to walk your dog but don't have time to do loose leash training, at least manage the situation. Get a Gentle Leader (or other brand of head collar) and use it. If your dog pulls in the head collar, circle him until he's paying attention before walking on. Then, when you do have time to train, work on walking on a loose leash with a regular collar. The "on and off" game works well for dogs of this age too—especially if you can work in a place where you can release your dog to really run and "get the ya-yas out." Once all the "ya-yas" are out of your dog, she will be capable of working for a longer, more concerted period of time.

Note: If you have an adolescent dog, you must have a place to go where he can run and get some physical exercise. A walk at human speed simply isn't good enough, and expecting an adolescent dog to pay attention and walk nicely before he has had a chance to work off some of his energy is setting you both up for failure.

Adult dogs (three years and older): At some point after three years, dogs begin to settle into adulthood. This is when you can take long walks and reasonably expect your dog to walk quietly—*if* you have built a reinforcement history. "On and off" is still a useful concept, but remember that adults still need exercise and the occasional romp.

No matter what your dog's age, there are three keys to teaching loose leash walking: getting (and keeping) his attention, reinforcing him for walking next to you (or slightly ahead, if that's acceptable to you), and choosing the right troubleshooting techniques for a given situation to discourage pulling.

Attention

First you need to teach your dog to focus on you in distracting situation. If your dog is far out in front of you, or sniffing or looking around, you haven't got his attention. Can you get it? Always? If not, you need to work on that. It's the single most crucial behavior you can possibly teach, because if you can't get your dog's attention you can't train for any other behavior.

If you lose your dog's attention the moment you step out the door, you're not yet ready to work on loose leash walking during your regular excursions. Teach attention first, and in the meantime manage the situation with a head halter, or find an alternative for exercise and "potty" walks.

Practicing Off-leash to Capture the Behavior You Want

Why practice loose leash walking without the leash? The leash is a tether for safety in case of emergency. It's not a guide to hold the dog in position. The goal is to teach the dog to walk in the proper place relative to you, so what difference does it make if you're using a leash or not?

Practicing off-leash walking is easy: just click and treat every time the dog shows up in the heel position—next to you on your left side. Don't pat your leg or call him.

Success Story

One of my first "ah-ha" moments came from one of the most basic concepts in Jean Donaldson's *The Culture Clash:* "Dogs do what works." What a simple concept, and yet it changed the entire way I approached living with my dog.

Brady wouldn't do something if it didn't "work" for her—that is, if she didn't get something out of it. She pulled on the leash because it got her there faster. She jumped up because it got her the attention she wanted. She growled and snapped at strangers who came in the house because it made them back off when she was uncomfortable. My challenge, then, was not to jerk on her leash when she pulled or yell "no" or "become the alpha dog" to scare her out of these behaviors. It was at that moment I realized my job was to find out how to make the behaviors *I* wanted "work" for her.

Keeping the leash loose "works" because she gets to GO only when the leash is loose—suddenly pulling didn't work any longer. Sitting pretty when greeting gets attention; jumping up doesn't. Strange people coming in the front door now mean great treats, and remaining in a down-stay on the rug away from the front door means those strange people don't get in her personal space too quickly, so she doesn't feel threatened and doesn't have to snap.

The other "ah-ha" moment came when I learned that I had to figure out and offer what motivated *her*, because treats didn't do it most of the time. For example, she wasn't interested in any food in any way, shape, or form when we were walking. For her, getting to GO was the motivator to offer a loose leash walk. I implemented "be a tree" and "penalty yards," with the reward being that we got to *go forward*, and clever girl that she is, it only took one session to *eliminate* pulling.

Cheryl Jarvis, Tempe, AZ

Just wander around and click and treat when he happens to be in the right place. Make that spot at your left side the most reinforcing place in the world.

Practice in the house. Practice in a fenced yard. Practice in a fenced tennis court. Practice anywhere it's both safe to let your dog off leash *and* quiet and contained enough that he's not going to forget about you completely. (Remember, you're supposed to be practicing attention too. You might get your dog focused on you and then practice off-leash walking.)

Building a Habit

Whenever you walk your dog, you have three techniques available—building a habit, "Be a Tree," and the use of environmental rewards—for teaching loose leash etiquette. Choose the right one for the situation you're in, and your dog will learn quickly.

The first of these techniques—building a habit—couldn't be more straightforward: simply reinforce your dog for walking in the correct position.

But don't skimp on this step. You don't even have to click—just shovel her treats when she's doing it right. Make by your side the best place to be. How long do you have to do this? Until it's a habit. If the dog is wandering off, tripping you, pulling to sniff a bush, etc., it isn't a habit. Deliver your dog's dinner, piece by piece, morsel by morsel, whenever you go on "walkies" until the habit of staying near you is ingrained.

In the beginning, you might—literally—feed the dog for every step in heel position. As she catches on, however, you'll want to space out your treats. Do this gradually. Don't rush! If you lose your dog's attention, you're going too fast. As you increase the number of steps (or number of seconds) between treats, be variable in terms of timing. If you always make your dog wait a certain number of steps before there's a chance for reinforcement, he'll start wandering while you're taking those steps.

"Be a Tree"

Use this method when the dog is pulling out of exuberance or when he simply wants to move faster than you do. Do not use it when he is pulling toward something specific.

Teach your dog it's not worth his trouble to go to the end of the leash. The basic idea is simple: never, ever take another step if the dog is in front of you. Stop moving. Freeze.

Wait until the leash becomes slack again then click and continue the walk. The leash going slack is only the first criterion, however, on the way to your goal.

Once your dog is actively offering a loose leash in the situation described above, increase your reinforcement criteria:

1. Click when the leash becomes slack or when the dog glances at you.

2. Click only when the dog turns his head toward you.

3. Click when the dog turns to face you.

4. Click when the dog takes a step toward you.

5. Click when the dog returns all the way to you.

6. Click when the dog returns to heel position.

How fast you can progress depends on the dog, the environment, how well you've done on your attention training, and whether you've given the dog the (needed) opportunity to both explore and get the ya-ya's out. The rule of thumb I use is to move to the next criterion only when the dog is actively offering the behavior that meets the current one within a reasonable amount of time. (Standing at the end of the leash for five seconds and then turning isn't good enough to progress, for example.)

The success of "Be a Tree" is dependent upon several factors:

• *Maintaining a high rate of reinforcement when the dog is in correct position.* Failing to do this is one of the biggest mistakes trainers make. If you forget to maintain a high rate of reinforcement for staying in correct position, your dog will quickly figure out that going to the end of the leash and back is the best way to get a treat.

• *Resisting the temptation to increase your criteria before the dog is actively offering behavior that meets the current criteria.* If the dog wanders to the end of the leash and spends five or ten seconds staring at something before turning to look at you, you are not ready to increase the criteria.

- *Always, always, always deliver the reinforcement when he's in the correct position, preferably in heel position.* Click for whatever criterion you've reached and then, if necessary, lure the dog back into the correct position before delivering the treat. Teach your dog that treats only come in that position—and that they are available freely once he's there.

Using Environmental Rewards

Use this technique when your dog is pulling toward something specific. *Most pulling is this type of pulling.*

Teach your dog that you are the giver of all environmental rewards. She gets excited and pulls on the leash because there's neat stuff out there. That's not a bad thing. Just take the time to teach her that access to all that stuff depends on her own behavior.

In this technique the dog learns that she gets what she wants by walking on a loose leash *and she loses what she wants when she pulls.* "Walk nicely to the bush and you can sniff. Whoops! You lunged, let's walk back to the starting point and try again."

Think of the environmental rewards as just that—rewards. If the dog does what you want, she gets to do what she wants—sniff, mark, greet people, greet other dogs, etc. But if she pulls you will immediately begin walking backwards.

A Few Final Words

Remember, you need to walk your dog on the leash—most likely more than once a day—and she's learning every step she takes. If you aren't reinforcing her for walking in the correct position, she's getting her reinforcement elsewhere—and I guarantee it's working against you. Be proactive.

Yep, it's a *lot* of work, but once you've built a habit it gets easier.

How do I train my dog to stay?

"Stay" means different things to different people. Some people want their dog to remain in place, but don't care if the dog shifts positions. Other people want their dog to hold a specific position the entire time. Here we'll address the first situation.

To teach a dog to stay in a certain place, use a boundary. When you use this method, the concept isn't "don't move" but rather "stay on the mat" or "stay on top of the table." Staying within a boundary is a concept most dogs learn quite easily!

This behavior is less strict than most. The dog is allowed to move around within the boundary as long as she remains quiet. If you make silence a condition of the behavior from the beginning, your dog will never develop the habit of whining or barking during stays.

As with other behaviors, you need to have clear criteria for each repetition. You'll need to add elements such as duration, distance, and distractions one at a time and gradually, increasing your criteria only when the dog demonstrates fluency at the current level. During training, if the dog crosses the boundary or makes noise before she has met your criteria, count that repetition as an error.

Tips for Success
- Train duration before distance. Work close to the dog at first, and add distance after she's demonstrating a grasp of the concept.

- Start with, literally, a second, and add more duration gradually. Long stays often fall apart because not enough time was spent solidifying the concept in the early stages.

- Reinforce with high value reinforcers during the stay. When you click and release, treat with a lower value reinforcer. You want your dog to look forward to the stay, not the release.

see also

Should I keep records? **page 90**

When and how do I add the cue? **page 93**

My dog is responding slowly to the cue. How can I get a faster response? **page 95**

When and how do I fade the clicker? **page 97**

How do I add duration to a behavior? **page98**

How do I add distance to a behavior? **page 100**

How do I train against distractions? **page 101**

How do I generalize to different locations and situations? **page 103**

Are clicker-trained behaviors reliable? **page 106**

- Add small distractions before you add distance. For example, wave your arms, jump up and down, circle the dog, put food on the floor (and quickly remove it if the dog breaks the stay), or bounce a ball.

- Keep records. Then you'll know for sure how reliable your dog is in a specific location, with a specific duration, distance, or distraction.

My dog pulls on leash,
and a friend recommended a head halter. Unfortunately, my dog hates it! What do I do?

I've never met a dog who truly liked wearing a head halter, but that doesn't mean the dog has to hate it. Think back to when your dog was a pup. He didn't like the collar or the leash in the beginning either, did he? But as he got used to them, he accepted that they were things to be tolerated. Dogs can learn to tolerate head halters in much the same way.

When you first get the head halter, introduce it slowly and make putting it on a happy event. Go slowly.

1. See the head halter. Click and treat.

2. Head halter touches his body. Click and treat.

3. Head halter touches his head. Click and treat.

4. Head halter slips over his nose. Click and treat.

And so on, until you can put the halter on. If he's struggling, you're moving too fast.

Once you've gotten the halter on your dog with little or no fuss, shovel yummy (tiny) treats for five seconds. Then take the halter off without any fanfare—all praise and treats stop when the head halter comes off. In the beginning keep your rate of reinforcement high enough that your dog doesn't have time to paw at his face. Over time, as he begins to accept the halter, you can begin extending the time between treats.

Your own attitude about the halter will have a lot to do with how your dog perceives it. If you hate using it and get tense and serious when you bring it out, of course your dog is going to be concerned. When you get out the head halter, act as though you've brought out your favorite party game. Be upbeat and happy. Let your dog know how lucky he is to get to wear such a fine device!

Associate the head halter with every fun experience, not just walks. Dinner. Training. Games. Have your dog "get dressed" for the occasion! Do lots and lots of short, short sessions, so he'll form a positive association. When you do begin to venture outside, make sure to keep the rate of reinforcement high. Keep your pup moving and keep the treats flowing. Don't give him a chance to worry about that weird thing on his face!

How do I crate train my dog?

see also

Do my dog's emotions play any part in training? **page 50**

How do I add duration to a behavior? **page 98**

How do I handle fearful behavior? **page 156**

A crate is a container large enough that your dog can comfortably stand or lie down in it when he's full grown, with a door you can shut to keep him in. Crate training can save your sanity and help you set your dog up for other training successes by managing his environment when you're not there to reinforce desired behavior. Unfortunately, many dog owners rush the process and end up with a set of different problems.

Introducing the Crate

The crate needs to be introduced as a place where good things happen. Forcing a dog into a crate is definitely not the way to create a good association.

The first day you get your dog, begin shaping the behavior of going into the crate on his own. Reinforce him for:

1. looking at the crate

2. taking a step toward the crate

3. sniffing the crate

4. putting his head through the door

5. putting one foot in, then two feet

6. going in to explore the crate

7. staying quiet when you shut the door

Reinforce this good experience by having other good things happen while your dog's in the crate. After you've shaped the pup to go in, feed him his dinner there. Give him a stuffed Kong toy or a marrow bone to play with in the crate. When he's ready for bed, wait until he's nearly asleep before putting him in, and then sit with him, stroking him, for several minutes.

Teaching the Dog to Spend Time Alone

It's a fact of life that our dogs have to be alone sometimes. For working families, the dog is often alone for most of the day. Even if you work at home, there are times you have to go out without your dog. Unfortunately, being left alone isn't natural to a dog. An abandoned puppy would die, and your pup instinctively understands that. He doesn't know you're just going to bed. He doesn't know you're going to work and will be back later. He doesn't know you're just going to the mailbox. He only knows he's being left alone.

The best time to start teaching the pup to accept being alone in his crate is when he's sleepy or when he's in the mood to be distracted by a meal, a bone, or a toy. The worst time to work on this behavior is when the pup is over-excited, in the mood to play, or has just woken up from a long nap.

1. Put the pup in the crate with something to occupy him, and shut the door.

2. Very matter-of-factly go about your business. For the first minute or so, stay in the room with the pup. If he looks for you, go over, open the door, and pet him for a few seconds. Then close the door and go about your business again. Repeat until he gets interested in his toy or settles to nap. Go to him only when he is quiet. Do not reinforce whining, crying, or barking with attention.

3. When the pup is distracted, leave the room. After thirty seconds, return. If he's looking for you, go over, open the door, and reassure him that you always come back. Repeat until he takes little notice of you coming and going.

4. Increase your time out of the room to one minute.

5. If the pup drops off to sleep, leave him alone until he wakes from his nap, then immediately take him out to potty.

6. If the pup finishes with his toy and doesn't settle for a nap, end the session with a potty break.

7. In later sessions, you'll be able to gradually increase your time away from the pup. Frequent trips back reassure the pup that you do come back.

If you're lucky enough to have time off when you get your pup or if you work in your home, take advantage of a pup's frequent nap times to teach him to feel secure alone in his crate. Putting sleepy pups in crates, Virginia trainer Victoria Farrington points out, conditions them to associate their crates with sleep. Thus they're more likely to relax or even snooze when crated throughout their lives.

Using the Crate

Once you acclimate your dog to the crate, use it correctly to maintain the dog's positive association:

- Make the crate a pleasant place to be. Find a treat—a particular stuffed Kong or a raw marrow bone—that your dog particularly loves. Give your dog that treat only as reinforcement for going into his crate on cue. Feed him the crate.

- Encourage your dog to nap in his crate. Carry sleepy puppies to their crates.

- Put a nighttime crate in your bedroom, so your dog is close to his family at night instead of isolated.

- Put a daytime crate in the family room. Leave the door open when you're home. If he goes in voluntarily, reinforce him.

- Never use the crate for punishment.

- Crate puppies less than eight months of age for no more than one hour for each month of their age. Crate dogs eight months of age or older no more than eight hours at one time. If the dog is crated while you're at work, he should not be crated when you're home, except for short periods when you absolutely cannot watch him and when you're sleeping.

- An over-tired pup may benefit from a "time out" in his crate. An over-excited, under-exercised pup will not. The crate is not a tool to contain puppy energy. Puppy energy needs to be properly expended. Otherwise, puppies put that energy into noisy, destructive behaviors.

• Crates are not substitute nannies. If you have a young or unreliable dog, watch him and train him. A crate doesn't teach a dog to make good decisions. It simply prevents him from making poor ones.

Solving Crating Problems

If your dog has a poor attitude toward the crate, go back to the beginning and progress through the steps outlined above at your dog's pace. Unfortunately, if your dog has formed a negative association toward the crate, it may take quite a bit of time to undo the damage. If you can, find a temporary alternative to crating while you retrain the behavior.

How can I train a behavior not covered here?
(Making a training plan.)

Before you train any behavior, you need to make a training plan. The first step is to define the behavior in detail.

- What will the finished behavior look like? Is this a precise behavior? If so, what distinct elements make it perfect?

- How will this behavior be cued? What kind of latency is required?

- Does this behavior have duration? Distance?

- Does your dog have to be in a particular place relative to you to perform this behavior? Are you always going to be sitting, standing, or lying down when you give the cue? If not, plan to spend times doing reps with both you and the dog in different positions.

- In what locations will the behavior be cued?

- What distractions might the dog face in those locations when performing the behavior?

- How reliable does this behavior have to be?

The definition of the behavior is a detailed description of where you want to go. The second step is to evaluate where you currently are. If this is a

Success Story

Via email, a friend with Scotties mentioned clicker training. I looked up the website she recommended, and ordered the clicker kit. When it came, I read the little booklet, and began clicking that same day. I still remember my sense of complete and utter amazement! I could get my dog to DO things!! I started with the "101 Things to do with a Box" exercise, and I couldn't believe that, without anything but a clicker and treats, I was able to get my dog to sit inside the box! I hadn't touched him, talked to him

or lured him in any way....I was ELATED!! Stuart earned his CD and CDX in eight months, from start to finish; it only took a month and a half to train him for the Novice exercises, and three months for Open. We're working on Utility now, and it is so exciting knowing that the world, previously not open to those of us with breeds like Scotties, is now our oyster!!

Amy Flanigan, Worthington, Ohio

brand-new behavior, that's easy—you're starting from scratch. If this is an in-progress behavior, evaluate the behavior for all of the above criteria. Keep records and let the data tell you exactly what your dog is capable of doing reliably.

The final step is to make a plan to get from where you are to where you want to be. Start with the behavior. Break it into responses and shape it to perfection. When it's exactly right, add the cue. Then one by one add elements like duration, distance, and distractions.

As you train, keep your training plans firmly in mind. Track your progress. Periodically review your plan, and revise the definition of the final behavior, if necessary. Don't stop working on the behavior until the actions your dog performs add up to a reliable mirror image of the behavior you described.

CHAPTER 12

Solving Problem Behavior

How do I stop destructive chewing?

see also

How do I solve problem behavior?
page 62

How do I crate train my dog?
page 140

How do I stop puppy mouthing?
(Bite inhibition training) **page 151**

Dogs chew. It's a natural, normal, *necessary* canine behavior, especially for puppies and young dogs. As a dog owner, your responsibility is to provide lots of acceptable chew toys and teach your dog to use them.

The following tips will help you get control of destructive chewing:

- Give your dog lots of acceptable chew toys. What constitutes "lots"? If you walk into a room where your dog spends lots of time and don't see at least three chew toys, you probably need more. Find out what she likes to chew, and make sure those toys are abundant. When you see your dog chewing on something acceptable, praise her! Let her know you approve of what she's doing. Don't take good behavior for granted.

- If you catch your dog chewing something inappropriate, interrupt her and redirect her to something acceptable. Be consistent—and persistent. There's no need to scold her for chewing the wrong thing.

- If your dog chews up something while you're gone, don't get angry when you get home; the dog won't associate your anger with her chewing. Put her in another room and clean up the mess without drawing undue attention to it.

- Puppy-proof your house. Pick up anything that might be chewed. Coat electrical cords and furniture legs with Bitter Apple or another bad-tasting substance. Do your best to make sure there's nothing inappropriate for puppies and adolescent dogs to chew.

- Watch your dog. Use doors and baby gates to keep her in the same room you are in. The dog can't sneak away and chew something if she's always under your watchful eye.

- When you're not available to watch her, either crate your dog or put her in a completely puppy-safe room. Set her up to succeed!

How do I stop my dog from barking?

Dogs bark for a number of reasons, some acceptable, some not. Common types of barking include the following:

- *Alert barking.* Dog barks to let you know he has seen or heard something out of the ordinary.

- *Defensive barking.* Dog barks to make something he is afraid of or doesn't like go away.

- *Attention barking.* Dog wants attention.

- *Frustration barking.* Dog is confused, frustrated, or stressed.

- *Boredom barking.* Dog barks to amuse himself.

Evaluate the Situation

When you deal with barking, it's important to look at the whole situation. Barking is sometimes a symptom of another problem—for example, fear, boredom, or stress. If you fix the problem, the symptom will likely go away. However, if you simply treat the symptom, the problem will just manifest itself in a different way—one which may be worse! Treat the *problem* not the *symptom*.

Define and Train an Alternative Behavior

Not all barking is symptomatic of an underlying problem. Often it's simple communication: "There's someone outside!" "I want to come in!" "I'm hungry!"

First, *listen* to your dog. Address the issue. Then determine whether barking was an appropriate response. Perhaps limited barking is all right under certain circumstances. Or perhaps you'd prefer to teach your dog an alternative way to communicate his needs. It's your responsibility to define an appropriate response in each situation.

For example, your dog alert barks when a car pulls into the driveway. First, listen to the dog and address the issue. Check to see what he's

see also

How do I solve problem behavior? **page 62**

How do I train against distractions? **page 101**

How do I handle fearful behavior? **page 156**

What is management? How do I "set my dog up for success"? **page 166**

What's the difference between punishment and extinction, which should I use, and why? **page 182**

Sometimes extinction doesn't work. Why not, and what should I do? **page 184**

barking at, thank him for bringing the situation to your attention, and reassure him you've got it under control. Then decide how you want him to react in the future when strangers drive in. Perhaps he may bark to alert you, but once he's done that you want him to be quiet. If that's the case, interrupt any further barking and cue another, *reinforceable* behavior.

Remove the Reinforcement for Unwanted Barking

Barking is, unfortunately, a self-reinforcing behavior, so waiting for the behavior to extinguish—even when another behavior is reinforced—is often futile. Therefore I recommend a combination of positive reinforcement and negative punishment.

If the dog continues to bark after being cued to do something else, or if the dog is barking for attention, one of the most effective responses is to remove what he wants. For example, if he wants to get out of the crate, stop moving or back away when he barks, then walk forward when he quiets down.

Manage the Environment

When you're not training, manage the environment so that barking isn't triggered and inadvertently reinforced. For example, if your dog barks when he's alone in the back yard, keep him inside except when you're able to go out with him. If your dog barks at passersby through the front window, either draw the blinds or keep the dog out of the front room except when you're there to address the problem.

When you're training, make sure inappropriate barking isn't rewarded—and that the preferred response is. Be proactive. Cue your preferred response before the barking is triggered.

How do I stop puppy mouthing? (Bite inhibition training)

Puppy mouthing is a hundred percent natural dog behavior. It's not dominance. It's not meanness. It's a puppy being a puppy, roughhousing with parents and littermates or with human substitutes. Rather than "no bite," I strongly, strongly urge you to teach your puppy *bite inhibition* instead. Bite inhibition means training for a "soft mouth." It teaches your pup to use his mouth gently with people.

How do I solve problem behavior?
page 62

How do I stop destructive chewing?
page 148

see also

Bite Inhibition Training

Dogs have one defense—their teeth. Every dog can bite. If frightened enough, or in pain or threatened, your dog *will* bite. That doesn't in any way make him a "bad" dog. It makes him a dog. It's your responsibility, therefore, to teach your dog that humans are fragile. If you teach your dog bite inhibition, that training will carry over even if he's later in a position where he feels forced to bite.

Dr. Ian Dunbar, an expert in the field, tells a story of a bite incident he had to assess. A golden retriever therapy dog was leaving a nursing home when his tail was accidentally shut in a car door. The owner went to help and the dog delivered four severe bites before she could react. Dunbar wasn't the least bit surprised by the dog's response. The dog got his tail shut in a car door! Of course he bit! What shocked Dunbar was that a dog with no bite inhibition training was being used as a therapy dog.

"But he's never bitten before." Of course not. And barring such an incident he probably never would have. But an accident is just that. An accident. Unpredicted. What if something similar had happened *in* the nursing home? A dog that's had bite inhibition training from puppyhood is less likely to cause serious damage even under severe provocation.

According to Ian Dunbar, there are four stages in bite inhibition training. The first two involve decreasing the force in the bites; the second two stages involve decreasing the frequency of the bites. The training must be done in that order. If you try to decrease the frequency first, the dog won't learn to soften his bite.

Because bite inhibition works by shaping natural play behavior, this kind of training should begin during your first, spontaneous interactions with your puppy and continue in more structured play/training sessions as he grows.

- *"No painful bites."* Ninety percent of puppies will stop mouthing in mid-bite if you give a high-pitched squeal or yelp. Then you praise the dog and reinforce by continuing to play. The other ten percent—and puppies who are tired or over-stimulated—will escalate their behavior instead of stopping. This requires you to confine the puppy or end the game. Remove all attention. Bite inhibition training does not require any added aversive—yelling, "popping" the dog on the nose or under the chin, shoving your hand down his throat, or spraying him with water.

- *Eliminate all pressure.* Gradually shape the dog to "gum you to death." (Service dog trainers do this routinely, because service dogs often have to use their mouths to manipulate human limbs.) Set a limit of how hard the dog can bite during play/training sessions. If he bites harder, yelp. Gradually set your limit for softer and softer bites. Move at a pace that ensures that the pup can be successful most of the time. A big jump in criteria is confusing and frustrating to the dog.

- *"When I say stop, you stop."* Teach cues for "take it," "leave it," and "drop it." Be able to both start and stop the game on your own terms.

- *"You may never touch a human with your muzzle unless invited."* Put the bite inhibition behaviors you have taught under complete stimulus control. Stimulus control means the behavior happens on cue and only on cue.

Coping with Puppy Mouthing in the Meantime

Although bite inhibition is a vital lesson, making it a training goal doesn't mean you have to tolerate constant puppy mouthing. Puppy teeth hurt!

Work on bite inhibition *only* when your pup is calm and you have time to sit on the floor and play gently. If the pup bites too hard, yelp. If he backs off, reinforce with calming pats and more interaction. If he gets too excited and bites harder, end the game immediately.

To end the game, you must be able to get away from the puppy with as little fuss or attention as possible. Even negative attention is attention. It's often helpful to have the puppy tethered, so you can simply move back out of his reach. Or play with him in a confined area and simply stand up and leave that space when he bites too hard.

The rest of the time, deal with mouthing by redirecting the puppy to acceptable chew toys. Literally surround yourself with chew toys, so you can stuff them in his mouth, one after the other, until he gets the message that you are not going to let him chew on you.

Puppy mouthing never requires anything more aversive than time outs or withdrawal of attention. Work on bite inhibition when you can, and at other times redirect or end the game. Physical aversives are confusing, unfair, and unnecessary.

How do I stop jumping?

Puppies greet adult dogs by licking their faces. When you bring a young puppy home, it's perfectly normal for her to jump up, trying hard to greet and elicit attention from you. When she's young, the jumping is cute. Then the pup grows larger and stronger, and her exuberant greetings aren't as cute anymore. Unfortunately, every time she was acknowledged when she jumped as a puppy, the behavior was reinforced—and most likely it continues to be reinforced one way or another, every time she jumps now.

> It's not enough to know what you want the dog not to do. You have to know what you want it to do instead. "I want my dog to ring a bell instead of scratching at the door." Versus "I don't want my dog to scratch at the door." "I want my dog to sit nicely for petting" versus "I don't want my dog to jump on people." It really does make a difference in training.
>
> Rachel M. Reams, Boston, MA

Fortunately, even if your dog has a jumping habit, there is hope. She jumps to get attention; therefore, you need to teach her an alternative way to get what she wants. Teach her to sit to be petted!

Start with your dog on leash. Go to a public place where people are likely to be friendly and want to pet your dog. When someone approaches, ask if he or she will help you. Or enlist a friend to meet you there. The process is simple. Instruct the person to move forward and pet your dog when her rear is on the ground—and to stop petting and back away when she stands up. Your dog will quickly figure out that her behavior controls what happens.

Be proactive. Don't get distracted and forget to cue the sit until the dog has already jumped. If you do, she will quickly chain the behavior—jump, then sit. Instead, watch your dog. As soon as you see someone approaching, cue the sit. If she jumps first, you weren't paying attention!

You can perform a similar exercise at home to teach doorway greetings. Does your dog mob you at the door? Stand outside the door and either cue—or simply wait for—her to sit. Reach for the doorknob and begin to open the door. The moment she springs up, close the door and drop your hand. When she sits, start again. As long as she's sitting, proceed forward. If she stands up, back up. Do this every time you come home, and she will quickly choose to sit when you come in.

Use a variation of this exercise to teach your dog to greet others at the door. Throw a beer, pizza, and dog-training party. Outline your plan to your friends and ask them to come in at fifteen-minute intervals. When they arrive, have them ring the bell and go in and out several times, paying attention to your dog only when she sits. Then send them to the living room to enjoy their food and drink and conversation. By the end of the evening your friends will have had a great time and your dog will be well on the way to considering visitors to be no big deal.

But what about people who don't want to help? Not every visitor who comes to your house has either the time or the inclination to help you train your dog. And it's unrealistic to expect to train for this behavior when you're trying to deal with clients or carpenters or formal dinner guests. So don't! Set your dog up to succeed at those times by crating her or shutting her in another room. Don't undo your training, or test your own patience, by letting your dog reinforce herself for jumping up.

How long will it take? It depends on how ingrained the habit was and how much effort you can put into training the new behavior. The best way to address this problem is never to let it start. If you have a new puppy, make a rule: no person may pet the puppy unless the puppy is sitting or lying down. Then make sure to follow that rule!

How do I solve problem behavior? **page 62**

What is management? How do I "set my dog up for success"? **page 166**

see also

How do I handle
fearful behavior?

Among dogs, minor uneasiness is first displayed subtly. The dog may be hesitant. He may lick his lips, yawn, glance away, or display other stress or "calming" signals. As the uneasiness increases into fear, the reluctance increases. The dog may try to hide or get away. He is unlikely to accept treats. If the dog is unable to get away, he may begin to display aggressive behavior, growling or snapping to warn the frightening thing away. Finally, he may attack to defend himself from what he perceives as a danger.

These stages may involve lots of clear signals, or the dog may seem to go from calm to aggressive without warning. Usually earlier, milder behavior in similar situations was ignored by well-meaning owners who disregarded their dog's signals of discomfort, not recognizing them as signs of a developing problem. Even worse, they may have suppressed these warning signals by punishing the dog for growling or "being rude." Instead of solving the problem, this just suppresses it until the stress builds and the dog eventually aggresses "out of the blue."

Whether the dog is simply tentative or is actively aggressing, the underlying problem is the same: the dog is fearful or otherwise uncomfortable with something in the situation. Treatment protocols generally call for a combination of counter-conditioning and desensitization. *Counter-conditioning* is a process for changing an emotional reaction by pairing low levels of a scary stimulus with higher levels of a positive stimulus. *Desensitization* involves increasing the level of a stimulus slowly enough that the subject's response to it remains constant at an acceptable level.

For example, say your rescue dog tends to react aggressively toward men. You might start by teaching your dog simply to tolerate the presence of a man. Ask a male friend to stand far enough away that your dog notices him but doesn't show any signs of stress. Shovel treats until your dog relaxes completely. Then have the man come a step or two closer until your dog notices him again. If your dog overtly reacts or refuses to take treats, you've moved too fast. Gradually, in later sessions, the man will be able to move closer and closer.

Once the dog is able to tolerate a male person within reasonable proximity, you might make all good things—dinner, attention, walks—contingent on the presence of a man. Gradually, through this counter-conditioning, your dog may come to view men as positive things.

Although training methodologies for treating fear-based aggression are extremely successful, they rely on exquisite criteria setting and timing, vigilant management, and a long-term devotion to correcting the problem. The best success comes when owners recognize the earliest signs of uneasiness and address the issue *before* it becomes a true problem.

If the behavior in question has progressed to the point of growling or aggression, seek the assistance of an experienced positive-methods trainer who can help you evaluate your specific situation and determine the best, safest way to proceed.

Food for Thought

Small dogs tend to feel more threatened by their environment—and with reason! More things can hurt them. So removing environmental pressures can be a key to teaching behaviors. I often work with "Sit" and "Down" on a table where the dog can still see its environment. I also teach "Stand for exam" on a table, for the same reason. When teaching fronts and heel positions, I get the behavior at some distance—where the dog can still see me—before bringing it in close to my body. I also sit on the floor a lot when shaping.

Natalie Bayless, Santa Barbara, CA

How do I handle aggression toward other dogs?

It seems to come out of nowhere: one moment two dogs are sniffing each other, then they're at each other's throats, snarling and biting. Terrifying. Violent. But is it problem aggression?

Dog Communication

Dogs have a rich canine vocabulary composed of body positions, sounds, and ritualized behaviors. From a wagging of the tail to a subtle lick of the lips to a snarling lunge, dogs greet each other, carry out daily interactions, and resolve conflicts.

Dogs have their own language and their own societal rules. Puppies begin learning this language and these rules in the litter from their dam and littermates. Singleton puppies and puppies who have lost their canine dam are often severely handicapped in this realm and may never be fluent in "dog speak."

The lessons continue beyond the litter. Puppies must be properly socialized during the first sixteen weeks of life, and that socialization includes interactions with well-socialized dogs of different breeds, colors, ages, and temperaments. Puppies need the opportunity to interact with dogs as *dogs*—off-leash and unrestrained.

The need for socialization doesn't end at sixteen weeks. As dogs age, they need to learn age-appropriate behaviors that only another dog can teach them. They need to learn social skills. In particular, they need to learn to greet other dogs appropriately. The enthusiastic dog who jumps on other dogs and "just wants to play" is behaving just as inappropriately as the dog who snaps and snarls at other dogs. Sometimes the ways in which dogs teach each other these lessons seem aggressive and violent, but they are usually appropriate, deserved, and *necessary*.

see also

How do I solve problem behavior?
page 62

How do I stop puppy mouthing? (Bite inhibition training) **page 151**

How do I handle fearful behavior?
page 156

How can I know when my dog is stressed, and what can I do?
page 170

Inappropriate Aggression

But where do you draw the line? When are dogs communicating and when are they fighting? If all dogs were properly socialized and had the opportunity to practice their dog-speak on a regular basis, inappropriate fights would be extremely rare. Unfortunately, too many dogs don't have enough of these opportunities and their interactions vary in levels of acceptability. How can you tell if you have a problem? Answer these two questions:

• How many fights has your dog been involved in?

• How many times did a fight result in a vet visit for one or both dogs?

A dog that has been in twenty fights with no significant injuries to either party is a considerably less serious problem than a dog that has been in two or three fights that all required vet trips afterward.

Drawing blood is caused by a lack of bite inhibition. Dogs must learn to control their bites. Once they do, they rarely do any damage to each other, even in what seems like a serious fight. Although snarling and biting is an accepted part of dog communication, injuring another dog is not because it would be detrimental to pack stability to risk injuring a hunter. Bite inhibition, then, is one of the first lessons a puppy learns from its dam and littermates. A dog who misses out on those lessons and who misses out on the opportunity for continued practice through early socialization with other canines is seriously handicapped.

Dogs who draw blood are not the only problem dogs, however. Any dog who launches into an aggressive display at the sight of another dog, who is unable to peacefully interact or coexist with other dogs, is a problem. In the vast majority of these cases, this

Success Story

For all those "out of control dogs," there is hope. My Bulldog, Hera, and I are a pretty good example. When she was about two years old, I realized she was getting serious in her lunging at other dogs. After she ran the length of a beach in order to jump on an old Lab who was throwing calming signals at her, I never let her off-leash outside the house again. Walks were getting fraught with peril.

I wanted a trainer who would work with us one on one and who wouldn't tell us to use a prong collar or to jerk the leash. I lucked out and found a very patient and skilled clicker trainer. I had all the usual resistance to clickers. I said that my hands were already full with leash and treats. My pockets were already full of plastic bags and more treats, and I had a water bottle for her slung over my shoulder by a strap. I'd given up being able to carry my coffee mugs on walks. No extra hands left for me... and now I was supposed to hold a clicker in my hand? What hand? Ah, but she was as skilled in training me as she was in training dogs.

We learned. We practiced nothing-in-life is free, and I learned that it wasn't mean—it gave my dog some control. We got clicker savvy. We can walk down a street and go for beach walks. Sometimes we have to turn and walk the other way, if the dog coming towards us is too scary. And all this because I learned how to tell her what I wanted ("click") and that doing what I want yields good treats. She controls the flow of treats. I think of the clicker as a translator. It tells her exactly what I liked and what will earn a treat. It's also a familiar sound that means good things, and when she's stressed and hears the clicker, it helps her relax. There's hope, take it from us... the "bad dog" in class and her novice owner!

Caryl-Rose Pofcher, Boston, MA

aggression is based on fear. Fear-based aggression can be treated using a combination of counter-conditioning and desensitization.

What about those cases that aren't based in fear? The good news is you don't have to diagnose precisely which emotion your dog is feeling. You need to know only that your dog isn't comfortable with the situation. The goal of counter-conditioning is to change a negative emotion—any negative emotion—into a more positive one. The goal of desensitization is to teach your dog to exert self-control in the presence of a certain stimulus.

Do counter-conditioning and desensitization work every time? The truth is, you can't make any dog like every other dog, but you can teach a dog to perform reliably in the presence of dogs he doesn't like. However, working in the presence of other dogs is not the same as living or cavorting with them unrestrained. In cases where counter-conditioning fails, the solution must be total management.

How do I handle aggression
toward children, strangers, or other people?

Nothing is more frightening to a dog owner than the possibility that his dog will injure another human being.

There's a stigma attached to dogs that bite, a label that dogs who have bitten are "bad." The reality is all dogs can—and will—bite under certain circumstances. A dog's teeth are its only defense, and if it is frightened, in pain, or feels threatened, it will defend itself. A dog that bites is not a bad dog. It's a dog. That said, unless it occurs in an extreme, predictable circumstance—for example, when the dog is injured—aggression toward people is cause for concern.

What is aggression? Is it a growl? A snap in the air? Do the dog's teeth have to touch the person? Do they have to draw blood? Dunbar developed a standard scale to judge the severity of a dog bite incident:

- *Level One:* The dog barks, lunges, no teeth on skin.

- *Level Two:* The dog's teeth touched the person, no puncture.

- *Level Three:* One to four holes from a single bite. All holes less than half the length of a single canine tooth.

- *Level Four:* Single bite, deep puncture (up to one and a half times the depth of a single canine tooth).

- *Level Five:* Multiple-bite attack or multiple attack incidents.

- *Level Six:* The bite tears out large portions of flesh.

The seriousness of a dog bite is determined by the damage done. A dog that bites but does no damage is more likely to be given another chance than a dog that severely injures someone, even if the bite was "understandable." Bite inhibition training, then, is a must for all dogs.

Above all, it's your responsibility as a dog owner to deal with any pattern of aggression before it becomes a serious problem. Too often people ignore escalating signs of fear and stress because they're afraid

see also

How do I solve problem behavior?
page 62

How do I stop puppy mouthing?
(Bite inhibition training) **page 151**

How do I handle fearful behavior?
page 156

How can I know when my dog is stressed, and what can I do?
page 170

of the stigma of having an "aggressive dog." However, if the symptoms are recognized and addressed early, the underlying problem may be resolved completely.

Once the problem becomes entrenched, however, the stakes are much higher. A dog that has learned to solve his problems by aggressing is a potential danger to others and a potential liability to his owner. Although aggression is treatable, it requires skill, management, time, and dedication. If you are worried about your dog's behavior toward other people, seek help from a professional, positive-methods trainer.

CHAPTER 13 Beyond Training

How do I build a good relationship with my dog?

see also

How can I establish myself as the "leader" in my home? **page 174**

As clicker trainer Sue Ailsby says, "There is no higher calling for any dog than to be a pet." Your dog may be a service dog, a search and rescue dog, a police dog, or a competition dog, but if our dogs are not also our pets, they are simply canine commodities.

At their best, the relationships between dogs and their owners are mutually beneficial. Dogs provide comfort, companionship, and security. We make them members of our pack, take care of all their needs, and give them a special part of our hearts.

Unfortunately, not all dogs and owners share that bond. Perhaps your dog is new to your home, or perhaps a less than happy history together has damaged your trust in each other. Happily, a good relationship can be established or rebuilt:

- Clearly define the rules that govern your household and teach your dog what you want him to do. Make desired choices highly reinforcing and manage your dog's environment to make undesirable choices impossible. Continually saying "no" is a sign you're not managing well enough—and you're not improving your relationship with your pet.

- Train your dog. Common obedience behaviors can be incorporated into everyday life to make it easier and more pleasant to live together. Fun behaviors like tricks give you and your dog a chance to play and laugh together.

- Spend quality time together. Give your pup a relaxing massage. Teach your dog to enjoy grooming. If you have more than one dog—particularly if you have two littermates—spend time with each one individually each day.

• Hand feed your dog. Ask for eye contact or stroke your dog before and during his meal to strengthen the association between you and this satisfying event. (If your dog is uncomfortable being touched while eating, skip this step until he's more secure and then gradually desensitize him to having people come near his food bowl.)

Food for Thought

My favorite thing about clicker training is that my dog teaches me at least as much as (if not more than) I am teaching her. She has taught me patience, humor, and the importance of living in the moment. I think I have discovered more about teaching and learning from her in the four short months I've had her than I have in the rest of my twenty-seven years put together. I have never been frustrated or angry or disappointed when training her because she won't let me—it is all a big wonderful game to her. She is smart and works so hard to get her click that she is learning faster than I ever could have imagined.

Lynn McNutt, Arlington, VA

What is management?
How do I "set my dog up for success"?

see also

How do I crate train my dog?
page 140

The world is a giant playground to your dog. It's full of all sorts of interesting, exciting things to interact with. Everything from a stick in the back yard to your brand-new leather shoes is a potential toy. Your dog doesn't know that some of those things are expensive or sentimentally valued or potentially dangerous.

Whenever you're there to watch your dog, you can keep her from getting into things she shouldn't and, more importantly, reinforce her for playing with the things she should. But what about those times when you can't watch your dog? That's where management comes in.

Simply put, your dog can't get into trouble if there's no trouble to get into. She can't chew the legs of the living room table if she's not in the living room. She can't chew your pillows/rug/shoes/ TV remote if she's not left with them unsupervised.

Set your dog up to succeed. If you can't watch her, make sure she's crated or kept in an area that is entirely dog-proofed. If she gets something she shouldn't, accept it as your oversight and vow to manage the environment better next time.

What are the practical uses of training in everyday life?

We train our dogs because training improves our relationships and makes it easier for our dogs to live in our households. However, it does no good to teach a dog to sit or lie down or come when called, if we don't use these behaviors to make our lives better. Basic obedience behaviors—stay, sit, down, and coming when called—are the building blocks for many other things you can teach:

- sit-stay at doorways instead of bolting through
- sit-stay when the doorbell rings and guests arrive
- ignore dropped food or forbidden "delicacies" found outside
- sit to be petted when people approach on walks
- down-stay or "settle" on a mat while the family eats dinner or while guests are present
- sit-stay while you prepare your dog's food
- stay calm while being handled by you, the vet, or a professional groomer
- walk politely on leash, no matter what the distraction
- remain calm when passing or being passed by other dogs
- come to you reliably in unexpected, possibly dangerous situations
- wait until cued to exit the car

Make a list of the ways you want to use common obedience behaviors. When do you wish you had more control over your dog? When do you wish your dog had more self-control? When would it be more pleasant for both of you if your dog did something different than he does now?

see also

How do I train my dog to sit?
page 124

How do I train my dog to lie down?
page 126

How do I train my dog to come when called? **page 128**

How do I train my dog to walk on a loose leash? **page 131**

How do I train my dog to stay?
page 137

How do I crate train my dog?
page 140

I want to train a behavior not covered here. How do I do it? (Making a training plan.) **page 144**

As you make your list, include an inventory of the conditions for each behavior. Does it need duration? Are there distractions? Does this behavior need to be generalized to lots of locations?

After you make your list, use it as a guide for training. It's a lot easier to train when you have a specific goal. Remember, it's easier for a dog to learn to do something rather than not to do something. If your dog is doing something you don't like, decide what you want him to do instead and train for that! Make the undesired behavior unrewarding and heavily reinforce the preferred behavior.

Success Story

Justin came to live with me at the age of two years. He had been handled with a lot of forcible restraint, when he was handled at all. He was wary of people, and avoided physical contact. In Justin's rehabilitation I see the best progress when I use not only the clicker, but also the clicker philosophy of giving the dog the choice to volunteer the desired behavior. In Justin's previous home, toenail care was accomplished by two strong adults hold-ing him down while a third ground his toenails. I began clicker training Justin to tolerate handling, giving him the choice to stay on the grooming platform or not. At first, he left after every time I touched him. Now, when he sees the clippers, he runs eagerly to our grooming spot and lies calmly while I clip and file all of his toenails.

Wendy S. Katz, Lexington, KY

My dog is constantly throwing behaviors at me,
even when we're not training. How can I stop this?

Why would you want to? You trained the behaviors in the first place because you liked them, because you wanted your dog to do them. Now he's freely offering those desired behaviors. That's a great thing!

But he's begging for treats!

Yes, he probably is. Clicker training teaches your dog to be an active part of the training process. He learns in training sessions how to "make" you click. He participates because you've made it worthwhile for him to participate. Now, by offering these previously reinforced behaviors, he's *communicating* with you.

Take advantage of the moment by holding an impromptu training session. Or if you don't have time to train or interact with your dog, either simply tell him "not now" and ignore the behaviors or give him something like a bone or a chew toy to occupy himself with.

When I start a training session, my dog "throws" all the behaviors he knows at me. Am I damaging these behaviors if I don't reinforce them? **page 69**

see also

How can I know when my dog is stressed, and what can I do about it?

see also

Do my dog's emotions play any part in training? **page 50**

How do I handle fearful behavior? **page 156**

Stress is a fact of life. Change causes stress—both good change and bad change.

We'd naturally expect major events in a dog's life—moving to a new house, changing owners—to be stressful, but even small changes like raising your criterion in a training session may cause some degree of stress. And although even a significant event may come and go quickly, its effects may take time to dissipate. Furthermore, within a given time period, multiple stressors will have a cumulative effect. Sometimes a dog may appear to "snap" and become aggressive "out of nowhere" over a seemingly minor incident, but on review it usually becomes clear that the stress has been building for some time, and this particular event represents the straw that broke the camel's back.

How can we prevent stress from building to that point? It seems that just about everything is stressful. Learning—training—is stressful. Good things, like going places and meeting new people and dogs, are stressful. We *can't* remove all stress from our dog's lives. Instead, we watch for subtle physical signals that tell us when a dog is becoming uncomfortable.

These signals have been dubbed calming signals by Norwegian canine behaviorist Turid Rugaas, who has produced a marvelous little booklet and video describing them. (See "Resources" at the end of this book.) They are part of the rich language of dog-speak that canines learn first in the litter. Although calming signals are used in dog-dog communication, dogs use them in human interactions as well.

When your dog begins to feel stressed, he will display calming signals—a lick of the lips, sniffing, a yawn, glancing away. This is the time for you to react and deal with the issue, whatever it is, before it escalates into a problem.

1. First, assess the situation:

   • What is stressing or frightening your dog? Are there multiple stressors or just one? Can you identify the stressor?

- How stable is the environment? Can you control your dog's access to and distance from the stressor(s)? Is a stressor likely to "pop up" and scare your dog further?

- How severe is your dog's reaction? Is he simply exhibiting occasional calming signals? Is he hesitant or overwhelmed? Will he accept treats?

2. If the reaction is very mild, the environment is relatively stable, and you can identify the stressors, you can remain in the situation and actively work on relaxing your dog. Be calm, and shovel treats until your dog visibly relaxes. If the dog is unable to take treats, he is too stressed and should be removed from the environment.

3. Your first responsibility is to your dog. If the reaction is more severe, the environment is chaotic and out of your control, or your dog's reaction is severe, remove your dog from the situation immediately. He cannot learn in this state, and the situation will only exacerbate his reaction.

4. Set up training situations where you can expose your dog to the stressor gradually and under controlled circumstances. Eventually, through counter-conditioning and desensitization, you can help your dog adapt to the stressor.

5. *Never* simply ignore the signals and assume your dog will "get used to it." Problem behavior often grows out of seemingly minor events. Address the issue now before it has a chance to become a problem.

How do I socialize a new puppy?

see also

Do my dog's emotions play any part in training? **page 50**

How do I handle fearful behavior? **page 156**

How can I know when my dog is stressed, and what can I do? **page 170**

The first sixteen weeks of a pup's life are a critical developmental period. In that sixteen weeks dogs are establishing foundations and behavioral patterns that will determine how they learn and adapt to new situations for the rest of their lives. Socialization to people and animals and exposure to a variety of stimuli are vital during this time.

Too little socialization and exploration can create a fearful dog insecure in unfamiliar circumstances. Unfortunately, overwhelming a pup with new experiences can have the same effect. A little forethought and planning—and this socialization procedure from trainer Tmara Goode—will help you achieve a good balance:

- Identify stimuli your dog will come into contact with on a regular basis. Consider types of people (different sexes, ages, and races), types of animals, locations, experiences, sights, sounds, smells, and textures.

- Identify stimuli your dog will come into contact with less frequently but that he is still likely to encounter in life—umbrellas, for example, or wheelchairs and crutches.

- Exposure to common stimuli will probably happen in everyday life. However, exposure to the less frequent stimuli needs to be planned. Set up situations where your dog is exposed to these things at his own pace.

The key is to allow the puppy to control the interaction and make his own decisions. Most pups will be at least a little wary of a new situation in the beginning, but given a chance to test and explore—and to retreat at will—they should quickly relax and accept the new stimuli.

If the pup refuses to engage at all, the intensity of the stimuli is too high. Remove him from the situation for now and think about its elements.

Perhaps the puppy was tired or there was simply too much going on at once. Or perhaps one particular thing made him uneasy. Try the following approaches:

- Arrange multiple exposures to the same situations or stimuli, particularly if the puppy was hesitant the first time he encountered them. The goal is completely calm, relaxed, confident interactions.

- Perform habituation exercises to desensitize your dog to specific stimuli. Put the suspect stimulus in a safe area where it will stand out. Bring the puppy into the area and let him off the leash. Let the puppy control the interaction. Don't interfere in his exploration.

Give your puppy lots of down time in places where he's comfortable and safe. Just relax or play with him or give him a massage. Monitor his overall stress level—not just during individual socialization events, but from event to event, day to day, and even week to week. Make sure he is well recovered from any one stressful event before exposing him to another stressor.

For example, after training your pup in the park for ten minutes one day, you take him home and he recovers, relaxing completely and easily. You have a more challenging outing planned for the next day, but that evening several boisterous friends stop by the house and your puppy gets over-stimulated. In the morning, he is a little "off" and appears stressed. Cancel the outing and perform a less stressful exercise at home.

Success Story

I ended up getting a puppy from a puppy mill situation. He had been in an elevated cage with his mother and littermates for the first seven weeks of his life. I thought I knew what I was getting into. For the first few weeks he whined constantly and tried to hide behind me. He just didn't know how to cope with anything new. But I kept persisting with clicking and treating for any bravery or calmness and exposing him to new people and environments on a daily basis. I enrolled him in a puppy clicker class, and gradually his fears have faded. Now, at seven months old, thanks to positive methods and using the clicker, no one would ever guess that he hasn't always been this outgoing and eager to meet new people, play with new dogs, and interact with new toys and environments. He has done a virtual 180.

Angela Pullano, Dayton, OH

How can I establish myself as the "leader" in my home?

see also

How do I solve problem behavior?
page 62

How do I build a good relationship
with my dog? **page 164**

What is management? How do I "set
my dog up for success"? **page 166**

In the past, people were quick to point to dominance as a motivation for most every canine problem behavior. In recent years, however, the trend has swung to the opposite extreme. Now dominance is often dismissed as a factor. In reality, the truth falls somewhere in the middle.

Dogs most definitely establish a hierarchical social structure amongst themselves, within their packs. If you have more than one dog, it's helpful to have an understanding of this aspect of social behavior of dogs.

Hierarchy and dominance are less helpful concepts in dog-human relationships. Dogs are patently aware that humans aren't dogs and quickly learn that dog rules no longer apply. In fact, they make heroic attempts to learn our sometimes arbitrary rules and to adapt to our ever-changing households.

That doesn't mean they're saints. Dogs are opportunistic, just as we are. They look for whatever they can do to get them what they want with the least amount of work, just like we do. Furthermore, if a tried-and-true method isn't getting results, they tend to escalate their behavior—which leads to what is often termed a struggle for dominance.

For example, traditional dominance theory states that a dog shouldn't sleep on the bed with its owners. The assumption is that dogs who sleep on the bed will come to perceive themselves as equal to their owners and will eventually challenge them for dominance. Indeed, there are examples of dogs who became quite aggressive and possessive toward the bed. However, this is almost always a learned behavior.

Typically, this type of problem has developed gradually. The human asked the dog to get off the bed or to move over; the dog didn't want to and resisted; the human didn't really care and gave in. Behavior reinforced. Next time the human was more serious. The dog resisted, but the human persisted. Hmmm. So the dog escalated his behavior and the human gave in again. Ah! So that was what was required to get his way. It didn't take long before the dog was growling or even snapping to get his way—and it was a completely learned behavior. If the owner had set, taught, and enforced simple rules—"off," "on," and "move over"—what's now a significant problem could have been avoided entirely.

Attaching the "dominance" label to a natural, normal behavior creates an unnecessarily adversarial relationship between you and your pet. Instead of trying to "show your dog who's boss" or find ways to make him respect you, find solutions that are mutually beneficial. Teach your dog that doing what you want gets him what he wants!

"Alpha" does not mean physically dominant. It means "in control of resources." To be "alpha," control those resources your dog wants. Make access to them contingent on behavior. Does your dog want to be fed? Great—ask him to sit first. Does he want to go outside? Sit first. Want to greet people? Sit first. Want to play a game? Sit first. If you are proactive enough to control the things your dogs want, you are alpha by definition.

Train your dog. Children, women, elderly people, handicapped people— all are capable of training a dog. But very few people indeed are capable of physical domination.

Reward polite behavior rather than pushy behavior. Reinforce your dog for sitting or lying quietly, not for pushing in for petting or treats. If you have more than one dog, the first dog to sit gets treated. Pulling on lead goes nowhere. Doors don't open until dogs are seated. You get what you reinforce!

Your job is to be a leader, not a boss and not a dictator. Leadership is a huge responsibility. Your job is to provide for all of your dog's needs— food, water, vet care, social interaction, and security. If you fail to provide what your dog needs, he will try his best to satisfy those needs on his own.

CHAPTER 14 Beyond Method: The Underlying Science

What is operant conditioning?

see also

What is clicker training? **page 2**

Are clicker training and operant conditioning the same thing? **page 181**

In the video "Patient Like the Chipmunks," Bob Bailey defines operant conditioning as both the science of explaining behavior and the powerful technology of changing it.

The principles of operant conditioning describe how animals learn. When trainers use operant conditioning, they apply the principles to obtain the results they want. Operant conditioning breaks learning into three parts:

• the stimulus that elicits behavior

• the actual behavior the animal does

• the consequence that occurs as a result of the behavior.

According to this theoretical framework, the consequence of a behavior determines whether it will be repeated or not in the future. If the consequence strengthens a behavior—causes it to occur more frequently—we say the behavior has been reinforced. Clicker trainers use *positive reinforcement* to teach new skills. On the other hand, behavior that leads to unpleasant consequences occurs less frequently. Trainers use *punishment* (as defined below) to suppress unwanted behaviors.

In either case, the consequence results from something being either added (+) or taken away (-) from the environment. This leads us to the definitions of four key operant conditioning terms.

• *Positive reinforcement (R+)* means adding something the animal will work for to strengthen (increase the frequency of) a behavior. For example, giving the dog a treat for sitting will increase the probability the dog will sit again.

• *Positive punishment (P+)* means adding something the animal will work to avoid in order to suppress (lessen the frequency of) a behavior. Jerking on the lead to stop a dog from jumping on people is an example of P+ used to suppress the behavior of jumping. Other common examples of P+ include yelling, nose taps, spanking, electric shock, and assorted "booby traps."

- *Negative reinforcement (R-)* means removing something the animal will work to avoid, in order to strengthen (increase the frequency of) a behavior. An ear pinch, traditionally used to train the forced retrieve, is a classic example of R-. The trainer pinches the ear until the dog opens its mouth, whereupon the trainer inserts the dumbbell. To reinforce taking the dumbbell, the trainer then releases (removes) the ear pinch. R- requires that an aversive first be applied or threatened in order for it to be removed.

- *Negative punishment (P-)* means taking away something the animal will work for, to suppress (lessen the frequency of) a behavior. For example, a dog jumps on you to get attention. By turning your back or leaving the room you apply P- by removing the attention he wants.

People commonly refer to the four principles of reinforcement and punishment as the "four quadrants of operant conditioning." That phrase is misleading in two ways.

First, it implies that all four principles are equally weighted or of equal use in a training program. In reality, punishment—particularly P+— has several drawbacks, some extreme, which make it inappropriate for most training issues. In addition, because an aversive must be applied or threatened before R- can occur, R- is also a poor choice.

Second, the quadrant description doesn't include a fifth principle of operant conditioning, one that clicker training makes particular use of. This is the principle of extinction. With extinction, a behavior is weakened through the absence of any kind of reinforcement. For example, if no one answers your knock at a door, you will eventually stop knocking. If a dog can't reach a dog biscuit on the other side of a fence, it will eventually stop trying. Because extinction doesn't have the drawbacks associated with punishment, clicker trainers use extinction to reduce or eliminate most unwanted behaviors.

A more accurate depiction of the relationship between the principles of operant conditioning and clicker training begins with the image of a pie. In clicker training, positive reinforcement is the largest piece, taking up perhaps two-thirds of the pie. The second largest piece is extinction. The third largest is negative punishment. Positive punishment and negative reinforcement are just two tiny slivers. The most important thing to note is that a complete, reliable training program can be composed entirely of R+, extinction, and, to a far lesser extent, P-.

Is it important to know these definitions? Yes, for two reasons.

First, it helps us understand each other much better. In everyday usage, the words "positive" and "negative" often mean good and bad. However, in operant conditioning and clicker training, they refer to something added or something taken away. "Punishment" is another word that carries strong connotations in everyday language, but in the context of operant conditioning, punishment means only that which suppresses the occurrence of a behavior.

Second, to clicker train without understanding the science makes clicker training nothing more than a cookbook full of recipes that may or may not work for your dog. Why? Because if you don't understand the underlying behavioral principles, you can't examine a training situation, determine why it is—or, more importantly, isn't—working, and adjust for your particular dog.

Are clicker training and operant conditioning the same thing?

This is a question much debated among trainers. Operant conditioning is based on five main principles, and all five are legitimate methods of changing behavior.

Karen Pryor, who coined the term "clicker training," defines clicker training as a subset of the principles of operant conditioning, using an event marker and including only positive reinforcement (R+), extinction, and to a much lesser extent, negative punishment (P-). The late Marian Breland Bailey, who, with her first husband, Keller Breland, brought operant conditioning out of the laboratory and pioneered and perfected the use of event markers in training, supported this definition.

Negative reinforcement (R-) and positive punishment (P+), though sometimes effective for changing behavior, have several possible drawbacks:

• They are difficult to apply correctly

• They may have unexpected side effects, including fear and aggression

• They generalize easily—but often inappropriately

• They generally rely on fear, pain, or intimidation

• They inhibit the animal's willingness to offer behavior.

This last issue—inhibiting the animal's willingness to offer behavior—makes P+ and R- most incompatible with clicker training. Clicker training can produce incredibly precise behaviors, but shaping these behaviors depends upon the dog's willingness to experiment, to offer a variety of responses, some right, some wrong. A dog that has been punished for mistakes isn't going to be anxious to try anything new.

Not all trainers agree with Pryor's definition. Many believe that clicker training and operant conditioning are synonymous. Others assume that adding an event marker (the clicker) to an otherwise compulsion-based training program is clicker training. If you're looking for a clicker trainer or class, speak with the trainer and, if possible, observe a session to determine if this person uses techniques you're comfortable with.

see also

What do I do when my dog makes a mistake? **page 54**

What do I do if my dog intentionally disobeys a known command? **page 55**

Shouldn't I tell my dog both what he does right and what he does wrong? **page 57**

What is punishment? **page 58**

Are aversives and punishers the same thing? **page 61**

What's the difference between punishment and extinction, which should I use, and why? **page 182**

What's the difference between
punishment and extinction? Which should I use and why?

Both punishment and extinction reduce the likelihood a behavior will occur again in the future. In punishment, something is either added or removed from the situation to cause an animal to change its behavior. In extinction, the change occurs simply from lack of reinforcement of any kind. Let's look at an example.

When you turn on your kitchen faucet, you expect water to come out. Each time you turn it on and get water, that behavior is reinforced, making it more likely you'll return to the faucet for water next time. One day you turn on the faucet and nothing happens. So you try again. Still nothing. You turn the faucet on further. You bang on it. You turn it off and on several times. Nothing.

The next day you try again. Nada. Depending on how well reinforced the "get water from the faucet" behavior was, you may keep trying for a while. Eventually, however, you'll stop. Occasionally, you may try again once or twice. If the faucet suddenly started working again, you might immediately begin using it regularly—or you might not, if you've found an alternative way of getting water.

This was an example of extinction. When you turned on the faucet, you didn't receive the reinforcement you expected. The water wasn't offered and taken away (negative punishment). Nor was something added to the situation to make you want to avoid the faucet—no electric shock when you touched it, no boiling hot water on your hand (positive punishment). You simply weren't reinforced.

When you weren't reinforced you altered your behavior. You tried again. You tried harder. You tried something a little different. These actions are characteristic of what behavioral scientists call extinction bursts. Later, once you stopped trying to get water from the faucet, you still occasionally tried again. That's known as spontaneous recovery: the behavior disappears for a while and then suddenly reappears. If reinforced, even behaviors that you haven't seen in a long time may be reestablished. However if you work through extinction bursts and moments of spontaneous recovery by continuing to ignore the undesired behavior and by strongly reinforcing an alternative behavior, extinction is an excellent way to get rid of undesirable behavior.

Punishment may seem to be equally effective but even if used correctly it may have side effects, including fear and aggression. In the vast majority of training situations, a combination of positive reinforcement and extinction will give you a suitably precise, reliable behavior.

Sometimes extinction doesn't work
Why not and what should I do?

see also

What can I use to reinforce my dog?
page 28

What if I can't offer a food treat or if my dog isn't interested in the reward I'm offering? **page 33**

How do I solve problem behavior? **page 62**

What is management? How do I "set my dog up for success"? **page 166**

What's the difference between punishment and extinction, which should I use, and why? **page 182**

Extinction works *only* if you are able to withhold reinforcement. Unfortunately, some behaviors are either self-reinforcing or are reinforced by the environment.

For example, dogs pull on leash because it gets them what they want—to go forward and interact with various things in the environment. Doing nothing and waiting for pulling on leash to extinguish is obviously an exercise in futility. Even adding treats for walking in heel position isn't likely to work on its own, because the best reward for a dog walking outdoors is the reinforcement of going forward, sniffing bushes, and greeting dogs and people—the things he's getting by pulling.

Clicker trainers use a combination of positive reinforcement, management, and negative punishment to solve problems that can't be solved through extinction. In the loose leash walking example, they use treats to make walking in correct position reinforcing. They use a head halter to manage the pulling. Since the dog is highly rewarded by the environment, they use it to their advantage. If the dog walks nicely to the bush, person, or dog he's interested in, they let him interact with them, but if he lunges forward, they might walk backwards away from those things.

What's a "no reward marker" (NRM)?

An NRM is intended as a signal to say "No, that isn't what I want—try again." From the operant conditioning perspective, it's intended to add a verbal cue to the process of extinction—"I'm going to ignore that behavior."

Intended to. Although NRMs aren't physical punishers, some dogs find them aversive and some dogs shut down when they receive NRMs. Unfortunately, what we intend is irrelevant. Furthermore, once you've added the verbal, you can't be certain whether the undesired behavior disappeared through extinction or through punishment.

Only the dog can determine if something is aversive. Some find an NRM aversive and some don't. Even if the dog you're training now takes the NRM in exactly the way you intend it, this doesn't mean the next dog will—and you'll have a hard habit of your own to break.

Humans are a verbal species, and it's natural for us to want to communicate verbally. However, we can use a verbal NRM, such as the word "wrong," if simply ignoring the behavior is confusing to the dog.

An NRM is unnecessary in most training situations. Extinction will occur if you simply keep your mouth shut and don't reinforce behavior you don't like. Keep it simple. Use continuous reinforcement and extinction.

see also

What is punishment? **page 58**

Are aversives and punishers the same thing? **page 61**

What's the difference between punishment and extinction, which should I use, and why? **page 182**

Continuous reinforcement, differential reinforcement, variable reinforcement—what do these terms mean? And how are they relevant for my training?

see also

How soon should I begin doing "two-fers" and "three-fers"? **page 39**

When a trainer trains, he defines what response is and isn't correct at any given moment. A "correct" sit in initial training may simply be a butt on the ground. Later, a correct sit may be tucked, square, and straight and require duration of five seconds. If the sit doesn't meet all of those criteria, it won't be reinforced. When the trainer reinforces some responses and not others, he is using differential reinforcement. All clicker training is based on differential reinforcement.

A trainer may choose to apply a specific schedule of reinforcement to his training. A schedule of reinforcement determines exactly how frequently a given behavior will be reinforced. Let's look at some specific definitions of these and related terms:

- *Reinforcer.* Something your dog is willing to work for in a given situation. Reinforcers do not have to be food treats and do not have to come from the trainer.

- *Continuous reinforcement.* This is the simplest type of differential reinforcement and the one used when shaping. The trainer reinforces every response that meets certain criteria. No correct response (as defined by the trainer) is taken for granted. This is what is recommended in this book. It's simple and adequate for the vast majority of training situations.

- *Interval reinforcement.* The trainer reinforces the dog according to a time schedule. If she's using a *fixed interval,* the trainer reinforces the first correct response that occurs after a specific period of time—for example, after one minute. In a *variable interval* scheme, the trainer reinforces the first correct response that occurs after varying periods of time within a certain timeframe. In interval training, the animal is reinforced according to the stated time schedule regardless of the quality or quantity of responses given during that timeframe. Note that intervals and duration are not synonymous. Duration is the length of time an animal performs the behavior. An interval schedule reinforces the first correct response after a specific period of time.

• *Ratio*. The trainer reinforces based on number of responses that meet his criterion. A *fixed ratio* means the trainer reinforces after a specific number of correct responses; two-fers and three-fers are examples of fixed ratios. If she's using a *variable ratio*, the trainer reinforces after varying numbers of correct responses. Often trainers who speak of a *variable schedule of reinforcement* (VSR) mean specifically a variable ratio.

Variable schedules of reinforcement are generally used for one of two reasons:

• to make a behavior you cannot reinforce regularly more resistant to extinction (for example, a search and rescue dog may have to search for hours without reinforcement).

• to reinforce a behavior that occurs at a high rate (it would be nearly impossible, for instance, to reinforce every step when teaching a dog to heel).

Should you use a VSR? The vast majority of pet and competition behaviors can be trained using continuous reinforcement. For the majority of trainers, a VSR adds an unnecessary level of complexity to their training program. If you have a reason to use a VSR, implement it after the behavior is fully shaped and strong.

> ## Food for Thought
>
> Bob Bailey talks about the rhythm of training and being hypnotized by the rhythm to one's detriment. I never did really "get" what he was talking about until one day when I was training BJ to touch a Plexiglas target that I held by one corner. There we are...
>
> Hold out target... touch... click... treat
>
> Hold out target... touch... click... treat
>
> Hold out target... touch... click... treat
>
> Hold out target... pause... click... treat
>
> Oops! I never noticed he didn't touch it because I was "into" the rhythm of clicking on a certain beat! So beware: don't do that!
>
> Helix Fairweather, Salem, OR

What is a
keep-going signal?

A keep-going signal is a cue—verbal or otherwise—given in the middle of a behavior to tell the dog she is doing the behavior correctly and should keep doing what she's doing.

Like no reward markers, keep-going signals represent an unnecessary level of complexity. If you increase your criteria for duration or distance only when your dog's performance of a behavior is sufficiently reliable at lower levels, or if you chain behaviors only when the individual parts of the chain are solid, you'll have no reason to give feedback in the middle of a behavior.

If you want to use a keep-going signal, condition a verbal signal—do not use the clicker. The meaning of the clicker should be consistent; it shouldn't end the behavior sometimes and not at other times. Don't make your dog waste energy trying to figure out what the click means this time. Instead keep training simple and consistent.

see also

What does the click mean? **page 18**

Does the click have to end the behavior? **page 21**

How do I train a chain of behaviors, such as a formal retrieve? **page 90**

How do I add duration to a behavior? **page 98**

How do I add distance to a behavior? **page 100**

What's a jackpot,
and when should I give one?

A jackpot is a mega-reward. For example, instead of giving out a single treat for a correct performance, the trainer gives a big treat—ten treats—all at once. Most trainers choose to do this after a particularly exceptional effort. Some choose to end all training sessions with a jackpot.

Do jackpots increase learning? Scientifically, the jury is still out. But jackpots certainly don't adversely affect performance, and they make the trainer feel good. So if you want to use a jackpot to mark a special event, go ahead!

What's the Premack principle?

see also

What can I use to reinforce my dog?
page 28

How do I train a chain of behaviors, such as a formal retrieve? **page 90**

The Premack principle states that a stronger response will reinforce a weaker one. What does this mean? It means that one behavior can be used to reinforce another. A "stronger" behavior is one that has been more highly reinforced or one that is preferred.

The idea that a more highly reinforced behavior can be used to reinforce a weaker behavior is the principle behind back-chaining. In back-chaining, individual behaviors are taught in reverse order and "chained" from the finish to the beginning. For example, imagine a sequence where the dog must go from point A to point B to point C, doing a behavior at each location. To take advantage of the Premack principle, the trainer would teach the behavior performed at point C first. Then he would train the dog to go from point B to point C, using the opportunity perform the behavior at point C to reinforce that behavior. Then he would train the behavior performed at point B, letting the last two parts of the chain reinforce that behavior. And so on.

The Premack principle also comes into play with regard to using environmental rewards. Watch your dog in a free choice situation and see what he likes to do, then use those things as rewards for other behaviors. Watch your dog at the park; what does he do? Mark a bush? Play with a dog? Chase a squirrel? Next time you're in the park, use the opportunity to do these preferred activities as reinforcement for doing what you ask first.

What's a satiation curve?

There's a continuum from absolutely-desperate-for-food starving to so-stuffed-I-can't-even-think-of-food full. A continuum. Food, or lack of food, moves you along that continuum.

What can I use to reinforce my dog?
page 28

see also

Neither extreme is conducive to training. A starving dog is so distracted by the sight or smell of food that he won't be able to concentrate on work. A dog who's stuffed to the gills isn't going to be the least bit interested in working for food or (most likely) anything else.

So you need to work somewhere in the middle of the continuum. The best time to work with food is when the dog is hungry but not starving; he will be interested in the food but not so interested he can't concentrate.

However, every bite of food you feed as a training treat moves you along that continuum toward full—toward satiation. A trainer has to be aware of this and plan accordingly. For example, service dog trainers work with their dogs throughout the day, not just once or twice. If they're using food in training, they need to know exactly how much they're feeding and they need to remain cognizant of how much training remains to be done that day. If they've filled the dog up by noon, they've shot half of their training day.

A dog trainer who trains less frequently still needs to keep the satiation curve in mind. Training after the dog eats his evening meal is poor planning. If the dog eats just one meal a day, training right before that meal might also be a bad idea because the dog may be too hungry to concentrate. It's up to you to find the right place on the curve.

What's the future of clicker training?

When the clicker first appeared on the dog training scene, many trainers proclaimed it a fad. As the years have passed, the popularity of the clicker has only grown. It can now be found in just about every dog-related sport or activity, and those clicker-trained dogs are not only participating—they're excelling.

Clicker training began as a grass roots movement in the dog training world. As such, there were no standards, no formal definitions of terms. As the popularity of the method increased, so did the variations. Even the definition of the term "clicker training" is contested. Some see the clicker only as a tool. Some a technology. Still others consider it less a technology than a philosophy that reaches beyond training into their everyday lives. Who's right? All of them.

Right or wrong, however, simply isn't the issue. The variations exist and will continue to exist. As clicker training moves out of the grass roots and into the mainstream, a level of standardization has to emerge. Concrete, industry-accepted definitions of the various types of clicker training must be established, not out of snobbery or a desire to exclude but instead to provide a common foundation for dialogue. Without definitions, there can be no communication.

Standardization aside, the future of clicker training looks bright. What began as a fad has blossomed into a movement. Whether people were initially attracted for ethical reasons or simply because it offered a solution for an "untrainable" dog, they're staying with it because it works quickly, efficiently, and humanely. Clicker training is here to stay.

Glossary

Aversive. Something the animal is willing to work to avoid.

Back-chaining. Training the last behavior in a chain first, then training the next-to-last behavior, then the behavior before that, and so on. Back-chaining takes advantage of the Premack principle.

Balanced training. A type of training using all five principles of operant conditioning and an event marker (clicker) to modify behavior. This type of training is better known as "combined training." Balanced training implies equal amounts of reinforcement and punishment. However, the fallout associated with punishment makes such a "balance" a poor training choice.

Behavior. Anything an animal does.

Behavior chain. A string of multiple behaviors elicited by a single cue. For example, in competition obedience on a single cue a dog will go out, pick up a dumbbell, return to the handler, and sit in front of her holding the dumbbell.

Bridging stimulus. An event marker that identifies the desired response and "bridges" the time between the response and the delivery of the primary reinforcer. The clicker is a bridging stimulus.

Calming signals. Subtle body signals used by dogs to indicate stress and to avoid or diffuse confrontation and aggression.

Chaining. The process of combining multiple behaviors into one continuous behavior with a single cue.

Classical conditioning. The process of associating a neutral stimulus with an involuntary response until the stimulus elicits the response.

Clicker. A toy noisemaker. Animal trainers make use of the clicker as an event marker to mark a desired response. The sound of the clicker is an excellent marker because it is unique, quick, and consistent.

Clicker training. A term coined by Karen Pryor and defined by her as a subset of operant conditioning using positive reinforcement, extinction, negative punishment, and an event marker to modify behavior.

Combined training. A type of training using all five principles of operant conditioning and a marker signal (clicker) to modify behavior.

Compulsion training. The traditional style of dog training, where the dog is modeled or otherwise compelled to perform the behavior and physically corrected for noncompliance.

Conditioned reinforcer. A neutral stimulus paired with a primary reinforcer until the neutral stimulus takes on the reinforcing properties of the primary. A clicker, after being repeatedly associated with a food treat or other reinforcer, becomes a conditioned reinforcer.

Consequence. The result of an action. Consequences frequently—but not always—affect future behavior, making the behavior more or less likely to occur. The five principles of operant conditioning describe the potential results.

Continuous reinforcement. The simplest schedule of reinforcement. Every desired response is reinforced.

Correction. A euphemism for the application of a physical aversive. The aversive is intended to communicate that the dog did something wrong. In some cases the trainer then guides the dog through the desired behavior. The application of an aversive followed by desired behavior is considered instructive, thus the euphemism "correction."

Counter-conditioning. Pairing one stimulus that evokes one response with another that evokes an opposite response, so that the first stimulus comes to evoke the second response. For example, a dog is afraid of men wearing hats. When a man wearing a hat approaches, the dog is repeatedly fed his favorite food. The goal is to replace the animal's apprehension with the pleasure elicited by the food. Counter-conditioning must be done gradually, however; if the process is rushed, the favorite food may take on the fear association instead.

Criteria. The specific, trainer-defined characteristics of a desired response in a training session. The trainer clicks at the instant the animal achieves each critereon. Criteria can include not only the physical behavior but elements like latency, duration, and distance.

Crossover dog. A dog that has previously been trained by a non-clicker method who is now being clicker trained.

Crossover trainer. A trainer who previously used non-clicker methods to train animals who is now clicker training.

Cue. A stimulus that elicits a behavior. Cues may be verbal, physical (i.e., a hand signal), or environmental (i.e., a curb may become a cue to sit if the dog is always cued to sit before crossing a road).

Desensitization. The process of increasing an animal's tolerance to a particular stimulus by gradually increasing the presence of the stimulus.

Differential reinforcement. Some responses are rewarded and others aren't. For example, a trainer wanting tucked sits would reward tucked sits and ignore all others. Differential reinforcement is not a schedule of reinforcement.

Environmental reinforcer. Anything in the environment that your dog wants. Trainers can use access to these things as powerful reinforcers for desired behavior. For example, say your dog wants to greet an approaching dog. You can ask for a behavior and then let your dog's compliance (or non-compliance) determine whether he gets to meet and greet.

Event marker. A signal used to mark desired behavior at the instant it occurs. The clicker is an event marker.

Extinction. The weakening of behavior through non-reinforcement or "ignoring" the behavior. In extinction, nothing is added or removed from the environment. For example, a treat lies on the other side of a fence. A dog reaches his paw under, but cannot reach the treat. Because reaching for the treat doesn't work—because it isn't reinforced through success—the dog will eventually quit reaching for the treat.

Extinction burst. A characteristic of extinction. If a previously reinforced behavior is not reinforced, the animal will increase the intensity or frequency of the behavior in an attempt to earn the reinforcement again. If the behavior is not reinforced it will diminish again after an extinction burst.

Fixed interval. A schedule of reinforcement in which the trainer reinforces a desired behavior after a specific period of time—for example, every minute.

Fixed ratio. A schedule of reinforcement in which the trainer reinforces a desired behavior after a specific number of responses. "Two-fers" and "three-fers" are examples of fixed ratios.

"Four quadrants of operant conditioning." An incorrect reference to the commonly seen chart illustrating the concepts of reinforcement and punishment. This description is misleading in two ways. It neglects to mention extinction, and it implies that all the principles of operant conditioning are of equal value in a training program.

Head halter. Similar to a horse's halter, a dog's head halter gives the trainer control of the dog's head, making it easier to manage a dog on leash until the dog has been taught to walk at the handler's side.

Interval reinforcement. The trainer reinforces according to a time schedule. In a fixed interval, the trainer reinforces the desired response after a specific period of time—for example, every minute. In a variable interval, the trainer reinforces after varying periods of time within a certain timeframe.

Jackpot. A "mega-reward" given after a particularly exceptional effort.

Keep–going signal (KGS). A signal—verbal or otherwise—given in the middle of a behavior to tell the dog he is doing the behavior correctly and should keep doing what he's doing. Keep going signals add an unnecessary level of complexity in training.

Latency. The time between the cue and the response. Ideally, that time is zero—or as close to immediate as possible.

Luring. A hands-off method of guiding the dog through a behavior. For example, a food lure can be used to guide a dog from a sit into a down. This is a common method of getting more complex behaviors. Lures are usually food, but they may also be target sticks or anything else the dog will follow. Trainers must take care to fade the lure early.

Modeling. A technique used in traditional training to get behavior. At the outset, the dog is physically guided—or otherwise compelled—into doing the behavior. Pushing a dog's rear into a sit is modeling. Clicker trainers don't use modeling because we want our dogs to be active participants in the training process, using their own brains to figure out what will earn them clicks.

Negative punishment (P-). Taking away something the animal will work for to suppress (lessen the frequency of) a behavior. For example, a dog jumps on you to get attention. By turning your back or leaving the room you apply P- by removing the attention he wants.

Negative reinforcement (R-). Removing something the animal will work to avoid to strengthen (increase the frequency of) a behavior. Heeling is traditionally taught through R-. The dog receives a "correction" when he walks anywhere except in heel position. Walking in heel position increases because that is the only "safe" place—because the threat of correction is removed by walking there. The key to R- is that an aversive must first be applied or threatened in order for it to be removed.

No Reward Marker (NRM). Intended to be a signal to say, "No, that isn't what I want—try again." From the OC perspective, it's intended to add a verbal cue to extinction. However, once something has been added to the situation, it's impossible to know whether a change occurred through extinction or punishment. No reward markers usually represent an unnecessary level of complexity in a training program.

Operant conditioning. The process of changing an animal's response to a certain stimulus by manipulating the consequences that immediately follow the response. The five principles of operant conditioning were developed by B.F. Skinner. Clicker training is a subset of operant conditioning, using only positive reinforcement, extinction, and, to a lesser extent, negative punishment.

Permanent criteria. Criteria that are found in the final behavior. Permanent criteria should be trained to a higher level of reliability than temporary criteria.

Positive punishment (P+). Adding something the animal will work to avoid to suppress (lessen the frequency of) a behavior. For example, jerking on the lead to stop a dog from jumping on someone is P+ used to suppress the behavior of jumping. Other common examples of P+ include yelling, nose taps, spanking, electric shock, and assorted "booby traps."

Positive reinforcement (R+). Adding something the animal will work for to strengthen (increase the frequency of) a behavior. For example, giving the dog a treat for sitting in order to increase the probability that the dog will sit again.

Premack principle. A theory stating that a stronger response or a preferred response will reinforce a weaker response.

Primary reinforcer. A reinforcer that the animal is born needing. Food, water, and sex are primary reinforcers.

Proofing. Teaching your dog to perform a behavior in the presence of distractions.

Punishment. In operant conditioning, a consequence to a behavior in which something is added to or removed from the situation to make the behavior less likely to occur in the future.

Rate of reinforcement. The number of reinforcers given for desired responses in a specific period of time. A high rate of reinforcement is critical to training success.

Ratio. A schedule of reinforcement in which the trainer reinforces desired behavior based on the number of responses. In a fixed ratio, the trainer reinforces the first "correct" response after a specific number of correct responses. "Two-fers" and "three-fers" are examples of fixed ratios. In a variable ratio reinforcement schedule, the trainer reinforces the first correct response after varying numbers of correct responses.

Reinforcement. In operant conditioning, a consequence to a behavior in which something is added to or removed from the situation to make the behavior more likely to occur in the future.

Reinforcer. Anything dog will work to obtain.

Release word. A word that signals the end of a behavior. After a behavior is strong and on cue, clicker trainers replace the clicker with a release word.

Secondary reinforcer. A conditioned reinforcer. A reinforcer the animal is not born needing. Secondary reinforcers may be as or even more powerful than a primary reinforcer.

Spontaneous recovery. A characteristic of extinction in which a behavior that was thought to be extinct unexpectedly reappears. If the trainer ensures that the behavior is not reinforced, it will disappear again quickly.

Stimulus. A change in the environment. If the stimulus has no effect on the animal, it is a neutral stimulus. A stimulus that stands out in the environment—that the animal notices more than other environmental stimuli—is a salient stimulus. A stimulus that causes a change of state in the animal—for example, causes him to perform a specific behavior—is a discriminative stimulus.

Target. Something the animal is taught to touch with some part of his body. A target is generally stationary.

Target stick. A mobile target the animal is taught to follow. Target sticks are often used as lures to shape behavior.

Temporary criteria. Criteria that are stepping stones to a final behavior that won't, in their current form, be present in the final behavior. Temporary criteria should be trained only to about 80 percent reliability before "making it harder." If a temporary criterion is reinforced for too long, the animal may be reluctant to change its behavior.

Three-fer. The animal has to perform three behaviors in order to earn one click and one treat.

Timing. The timing of the clicker. Ideally, the click should occur at exactly the same instant the target criterion is achieved. Timing is a mechanical skill and requires practice. The trainer must be able to recognize the behaviors that precede the target behavior in order to click at the very moment the target behavior occurs.

Traditional training. Compulsion training. Traditional training is characterized by modeling or luring to get the behavior and the use of negative reinforcement and positive punishment to "proof" it.

Training period. A pre-set period of time set aside for training. A training period may be composed of multiple training sessions.

Training session. Either a pre-set period of time or pre-set number of repetitions. Your criteria should remain constant during a single session. At the end of a training session, the trainer evaluates the animal's progress and decides whether to make the next session harder or stay at the same criteria.

Two-fer. The animal has to perform two behaviors in order to earn one click and one treat.

Variable interval. A schedule of reinforcement in which the trainer reinforces desired behavior after varying periods of time within a certain timeframe.

Variable ratio. A schedule of reinforcement in which the trainer reinforces desired behavior after varying numbers of "correct" responses.

Variable schedule of reinforcement (VSR). Technically, either a variable interval or variable ratio. However, most trainers use VSR to mean a variable ratio.

Recommended Books

Must-haves for all trainers and dog owners

Don't Shoot the Dog, by Karen Pryor

The Culture Clash, by Jean Donaldson

On Talking Terms with Dogs: Calming Signals, by Turid Rugaas

The Other End of the Leash, by Patricia McConnell

Clicker training books

Clicking with Your Dog: Step-By-Step in Pictures, by Peggy Tillman

Clicker Training for Obedience, by Morgan Spector

Click to Win, by Karen Pryor

Dog behavior

An Owner's Guide to Dog Behavior, by Ian Dunbar

Dogs: A Startling New Understanding of Canine Origin, Behavior, and Evolution, by Ray and Lorna Coppinger

I'll Be Home Soon!, by Patricia McConnell

The Cautious Canine, by Patricia McConnell

Feeling Outnumbered? How to Manage and Enjoy Your Multi-Dog Household, by Karen London and Patricia McConnell

Positive training, but not specifically clicker

Before You Get Your Puppy, by Ian Dunbar

After You Get Your Puppy, by Ian Dunbar

The Power of Positive Training, by Pat Miller

Advanced or scholarly texts

Coercion and Its Fallout, by Murray Sidman

Pet Behavior Protocols, by Suzanne Hetts

Animal Training: Successful Animal Management through Positive Reinforcement, by Ken Ramirez

Handbook of Applied Dog Behavior and Training (2 vols.), by Steven Linsday

Canine Aggression Workbook, by James O'Heare

Recommended Videos

Must-haves for all trainers and dog owners

"Patient Like the Chipmunks," by Bob and Marian Bailey—the history of operant conditioning outside of the laboratory.

"Calming Signals: What Your Dog Tells You," by Turid Rugaas

Clicker training videos

"Clicker Magic," by Karen Pryor

"Click and Go," by Deb Jones

"Click and Fix," by Deb Jones—a must-have for pet owners who want solid solutions to common problem behaviors.

"Take a Bow Wow!" (2 vols.), by Virginia Broitman and Sherri Lippman

Other video resources

http://www.puppyworks.com—Puppyworks hosts a variety of educational dog seminars and frequently has videos of these presentations for sale.

Advanced or scholarly videos

"Canine Behavior Program: Body Postures and Evaluating Behavioral Health," by Suzanne Hetts and Daniel Estep

Recommended Websites

Clicker training websites

www.clickersolutions.com

www.clickertraining.com

www.clickertales.com

www.travelvan.net/cgi-bin/marge/mainpage.pl
Find a clicker trainer in your area.

www.wagntrain.com/clicker_training.htm

www.dogpatch.org/obed/obpage4.cfm
Dogpatch's collection of clicker training links.

Recommended clicker training mailing lists

groups.yahoo.com/group/ClickerSolutions/
ClickerSolutions—positive solutions to training and behavior problems. A general list great for both beginners and advanced trainers.

groups.yahoo.com/group/Pos-4-ReactiveDogs/
A list for owners of reactive, fearful dogs.

groups.yahoo.com/group/clickteach/
A list for clicker training instructors.

groups.yahoo.com/group/OC-Assist-Dogs/
A list for people interested in clicker training service dogs.

groups.yahoo.com/group/PositiveGunDogs/
A list for people interested in clicker training retrievers and gun dogs.

groups.yahoo.com/group/spt
Start Puppy Training mailing list.

Index

Acknowledgements

I've wanted to be a writer since third grade, but it wasn't until the summer of 2001 that my wonderful husband, Jason, gave me the opportunity to pursue my dream. This book would not exist without Jason's generosity. By the same token, I want to thank Myella Karls, who gave me the courage to begin and persist, and Ashley Sharp, who believed in me until I could believe in myself. You three truly made this book—and my dream—possible. I love you!

Though writers tend to spend far too much time lost in a world of their own words and ideas, the process of writing a book is not a solitary one. It is a conglomeration of ideas and experiences. Thanks must go, first and foremost then, to Doug Johnson, who had the tedious job of reading my rough text, pointing out the holes, inconsistencies, and errors, and guiding my rewrite until every paragraph was accurate and clear. Thanks too to my ClickerSolutions list admins—Debbie Otero, Debi Davis, Carol Whitney, Denise Nord, Tmara Goode, Marge Morgan, and Jos Lermyte—who cheered and supported me every step of the way; to Gitta Vaughn, who read the first half of my manuscript and let me know that I was on the right track; and to Gale Pryor and Karen Pryor's Clicker Training™, who had faith in an unpublished writer.

Special thanks go to the members of the ClickerSolutions mailing list who asked the questions and constantly forced me to reevaluate and refine my answers. I would especially like to mention all of the members who submitted success stories, embarrassing training moments, and training tips: Anna Carolyn Abney, Tracie Barber, Laura Baugh, Natalie Bayless, Deb Boyken, Stacy Braslau-Schneck, Jo Butler, Cathi Cline, Robert Crosser, Debi Davis, Pamela Dennison, Suzy Dunkelman, Amy Dunphy, Lynda Edmondson, Helix Fairweather, Amy Flanigan, Tmara Goode, Laurie Graichen, Heidi Hansen, Cheryl Jarvis, Laura Kansanen, Greta Kaplan, Wendy Katz, Susan Kues, Val Leslie, Christina MacIntyre, Susan Mann, Lynn McNutt, Tamandra Michaels, Melissa Murray, Erica Nance, Jan Niemeyer, Anu Nieminen, Elaine Normandy, Gina O'Keefe, Gail Parker, Caryl-Rose Pofcher, Leandra Prior, Angela Pullano, Rachel Reams, Lyle Reed, Ellen Ryan, Peggy Schaefer, Francine Shacter, Terri Stilson, Michele Stone, Tara Tabler, Eva Thollander, Eileen Trethewey, Stephanie Weaver, Sally Wells, Nicole Wilde, Lisa Yanchunis, Katherine Yata, and Monica Zaworski.

Finally I want to thank all of the people—pet owners and professional trainers alike—who taught me how to train dogs using a system that is reinforcing for all involved. Most especially, I want to thank Bob Bailey and the late Marian Breland Bailey. You were my most influential teachers. You taught me more than the theory—you taught me the skills that make the theory a powerful vehicle for changing behavior. Deepest gratitude to you both.